Essential Skills for
SCALE MODELERS

AARON SKINNER

KALMBACH BOOKS

Kalmbach Books
21027 Crossroads Circle
Waukesha, Wisconsin 53186
www.Kalmbach.com/Books

All photos by the author or Kalmbach Books unless credited otherwise.

Published in 2011

15 14 13 12 11   1 2 3 4 5

This product is a Print on Demand format of the original book published by Kalmbach Publishing Company.

ISBN: 978-0-89024-791-4

Publisher's Cataloging-In-Publication Data

Skinner, Aaron.
  Essential skills for scale modelers / Aaron Skinner.

   p. : col. ill. ; cm. -- (FineScale modeler books) -- (Scale modeler's how-to guide)

   ISBN: 978-0-89024-791-4

   1. Models and modelmaking--Handbooks, manuals, etc. I. Title. II. Title: Scale modelers
III. Series: FineScale modeler books.

TT154 .S56 2011
688/.1

Contents

Building scale models is a rewarding hobby that connects you to history and provides an outlet for creativity. It's part exacting science and part art—and it's all fun.

Maybe you're new to modeling. Or maybe you built models as a kid, and as you got older, the distractions of dating, cars, athletics, college, career, military service, marriage, and/or children pushed this quiet hobby to the back burner. Now you've got some time to spare, and a hobby may be just the ticket. Whatever route you took to get here, this book is designed to give you some tips and techniques for building better models.

Through various projects, I'll show you how I do everything from clipping parts off a sprue to painting and gluing as well as working with materials that have become increasingly common such as photoetched metal and resin. You can follow along by acquiring the kits I used, or you can adapt the techniques to fit models you want to build.

Modeling improves with practice, and it is best learned by doing over and over again. Each model I build seems to be better than the next. Don't be afraid to try new things and push the envelope with each build. Just be patient with yourself. I can't tell you how many models I've screwed up by rushing to get done. Modeling is rarely good when you are in a hurry.

These techniques are what works for me, but they are not the be-all and end-all of modeling. I've been building models for more than 30 years, and I am still learning things. So let's learn a few things and have some fun.

Starting with THE BASICS

1

Skills

• Removing parts and cleanup
• Gluing
• Filling gaps
• Spray-painting

Armor modeling can be challenging. Some kits have hundreds of parts, including resin and photoetched metal, and difficult camouflage schemes. But basic kits offer a good introduction to the most important modeling skills, so they can be a good way to get started. For the first project in this book, I chose one of Trumpeter's 1/35 scale KV kits. It's a good choice because it has optional vinyl tracks and a single-color paint scheme.

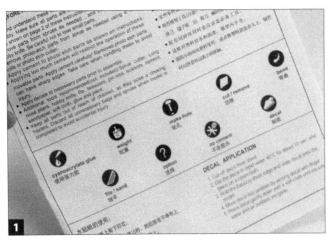

1 Before getting too deep into the kit, to avoid mistakes, make sure you understand all of the symbols in the instructions.

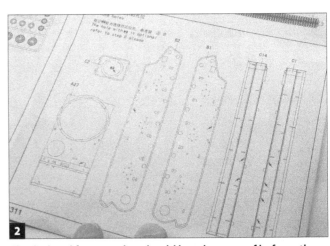

2 Check ahead for steps that should be taken care of before others, such as drilling holes.

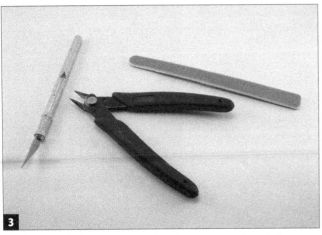

3 The basic tools for part removal and cleanup are, from left, a hobby knife, sprue cutter, and sanding stick.

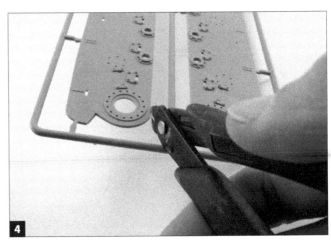

4 Keep the sprue cutter's flat side as close as possible to the part being removed for a cleaner cut and less sanding.

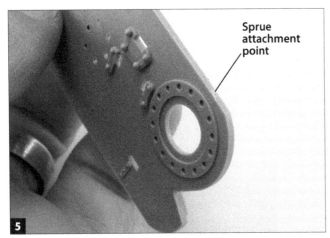

Sprue attachment point

5 There is always some remnant of the attachment point left.

6 Shave away the stub with a new No. 11 blade...

Make a plan. The first step for any build is opening the box and looking at the parts and the instructions. Kit designers frequently design instructions with a sequence that makes sense if you plan to simply build the model, but they don't take into account painting of detail parts or the need to leave delicate parts off to avoid breaking them during construction, sanding, and finishing. I've seen tank models that instruct you to add small parts such as grab handles before building the upper and lower hulls. Chances are those parts will get broken while cleaning up the joint between the major parts. The instructions in aircraft kits often show landing gear or pitot tubes being added at an early stage when they would be better left off until the model is painted.

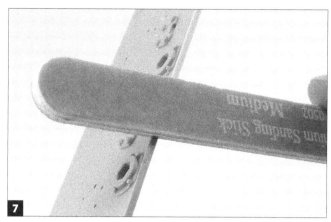

7

...and then finish the job with a sanding stick.

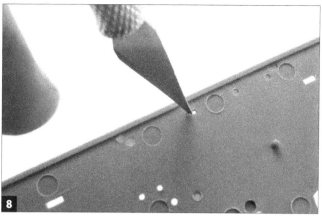

8

To open square locator holes on the hull side, I pierced the thin plastic on all four sides of the hole with the point of a knife from the back side.

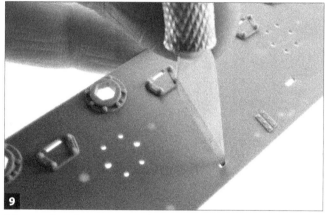

9

After turning the part over, I cleaned up the opening.

10

Dry- or test-fitting parts before gluing is important for discovering problems such as gaps all the way around the hull side.

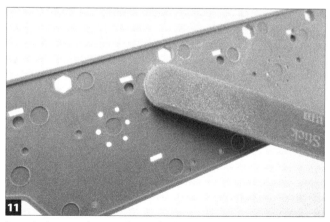

11

I sanded away ejector-pin marks (round depressions left in plastic as the parts are being extracted from the molding machine) on the back of a hull side.

12

Apply Testors Liquid Cement in preparation for attaching the hull sides.

As you look at the instructions, examine the steps and sequences indicated and think about any changes that might be appropriate. Trumpeter's KV is pretty well laid out, starting with the hull and suspension, followed by details, and then the turret. Familiarize yourself with the symbols used in the instructions to indicate special techniques. Some are self-explanatory, but others can be a little obtuse, **1**. Watch for optional parts; some kits allow you to build more than one variant of a vehicle. Also pay attention to places where you will need to open flashed-over locator holes, **2**. I can tell you from experience that it is much easier to open those before construction.

THE ABCs OF PAINT

Testors Model Master enamels (center) are widely available at hobby stores and come in a wide range of colors. Humbrol and Xtracolor are also good options, especially if you are building British subjects.

Model Master Acryl paints (left) are thin enough to airbrush out of the bottle. Tamiya paints airbrush beautifully but need to be thinned. Vallejo paints brush-paint beautifully. Xtracrylix features European colors and airbrush well.

Testors sells lacquers for car modeling (left) as well as metallics.

Wipe paint from threads to prevent lids from sticking. Excess buildup prevents a good seal and causes paint to dry out.

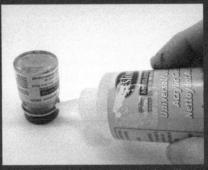

Letting thinner sit in the threads will usually free stuck paint lids.

Thinners come in many forms, but it's best to use the one recommended by the paint manufacturer.

Using the right kind of paint is essential for good-looking models. But stand in the paint aisle of a well-stocked hobby store, and it's easy to be overwhelmed. Besides hundreds of tiny bottles in all kinds of colors, there are different kinds of paint: enamel, acrylic, lacquer, and artist's oils. You're on your own when it comes to choosing colors, but let's talk about paint types, what they mean, and how to use them.

Enamels. The standard for model paint since the first plastic kits were produced, petroleum-based enamels are still widely available. They take longer to dry than acrylics, but that's not always a bad thing. Slower drying means the paint has more time to level out, so it's very easy to get a smooth finish. In addition to brush-painting, they're great for airbrushing: there's less chance of paint drying at the nozzle with enamels than acrylics, and the paint is less likely to dry on the way to the model. But slow drying means you have to wait longer between coats.

Acrylics. The new kid on the block, acrylic paints feature generally faster drying times, and they smell better than enamels. Not all acrylics are created equal. Some, such as craft paints, are truly water-based; others use alcohol or other chemicals as a base. Acrylic paints are more susceptible than enamels to surface contamination such as mold-release agents or skin oils. I clean plastic before any painting, but with acrylics, I wipe the surface with rubbing alcohol or Testors Plastic Prep. There are many more differences between acrylic paint brands than there are between enamels. Don't assume that what works with one brand works across all. Thinning ratios vary quite a bit, even from one color to another within a single brand.

Lacquers. Also solvent-based, lacquers are fast drying and thin. They are most commonly used as metallics and for car modeling. They tend to be very aggressive and will attack plastic, so use a primer or apply the paint in multiple thin layers.

Stirring and prep. Paint settles and separates when not in use. Most manufactur-

ers recommend stirring the paint to mix it, rather than shaking it. I usually use a combination of the two. You want to be sure the texture is consistent and that there are no lumps at the bottom of the jar. Dropping a couple of BBs into the jar as agitators helps mix the paint when shaking. Enamels tend to need more mixing than acrylics. Wipe paint from the lip of the container and off threads to prevent paint from gumming up the works and causing the lid to stick shut. If that happens, drip a little thinner into the lid's gap and let the bottle sit upside down for a few minutes. If you resort to using pliers, be careful—a lapful of German dark yellow isn't a great end to a modeling session.

Thinners. Most paints need to be thinned for airbrushing, and it's always a good idea to have thinner handy when brush-painting to keep the paint flowing nicely. Whatever type of paint you use, follow the manufacturer's instructions—usually found in tiny print on the bottle—when it comes to thinners and thinning ratios. Most brands have a matching thinner, and although it may be more expensive

Paint separates as it sits, leaving gooey globs in the bottom of the jar. Stirring and shaking, especially with BBs, will take care of the problem.

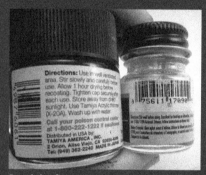

Read the fine print. Paint bottles are small as are the directions for thinning and airbrushing printed on the labels.

than a gallon of generic paint thinner at the paint store, you have peace of mind knowing it's going to work. If you decide to use a thinner or other additive not recommended, test it on something besides the model you've spent the last six months getting just right. The finish line is not the time for surprises. Don't add thinner straight to the original paint bottle and don't store thinned paint for more than a few days. Thinner will disturb the paint's balance of solvent, vehicle, and pigment, and the paint will become unusable.

Safety. Paints and thinners, even kinder, gentler acrylics, should be treated as poisons, and precautions should be taken. While it goes without saying that you're unlikely to drink paint (to be sure, don't keep thinner or paint in anything that can be mistaken for a drinking glass), inhaling the fumes can be just as harmful. Always paint in well ventilated environment and use a respirator when airbrushing.

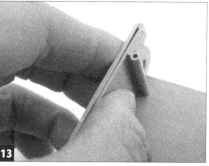

I checked the fit all the way around, and this gap might have been difficult to fix if it had gone unnoticed.

I removed the rear plate's mold seam with a few strokes of a sanding stick.

Rubber bands are perfect for holding parts together as the glue dries.

Removing parts. As a kid, I remember the glee I experienced bodily twisting parts off the sprue. When I was 8, big chunks of excess plastic or divots left from this removal method meant little on a model with a life expectancy of about two hours. As kits went from being toys to a serious hobby, I had to alter my methods.

The basic tools for removing parts from the tree are a hobby knife, side cutters (or sprue cutters), and sanding stick, **3**. See Chapter 2 for more information about these and other tools. For large, sturdy parts like the KV's hull sides, place

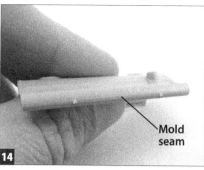

Mold seams are ridges of plastic left where mold parts meet during manufacture, and they are frequently found on round parts.

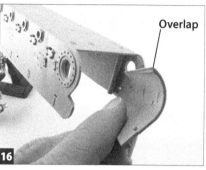

I thought the rear plate needed work until I noticed that it should extent slightly below the hull bottom.

Some of the kit's smaller parts had flash, thin plates of plastic caused when plastic leaks out of the mold, which is easy to remove with a hobby knife and sanding.

the flat side of the sprue cutter near the point where the attachment point meets the part and squeeze the jaws together, **4**. Even the closest cut leaves a small blemish that will be obvious on the finished model or will interfere with part's fit, **5**. To remove the excess plastic, start by trimming it with a sharp No. 11 blade, **6**. Be careful: it's easy to cut too deep and gouge the part. And never cut toward yourself—did I mention the blades should be sharp?

A few passes with a sanding stick will smooth the surface, **7**. Take care when

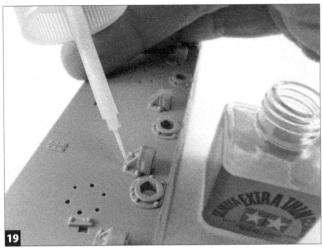

19 As you touch the brush to the gap, capillary action pulls Tamiya Extra Thin Liquid Cement into the join.

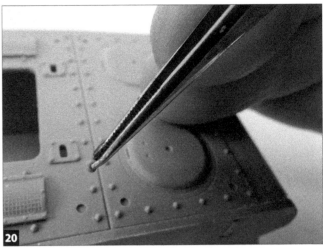

20 I used long, thin tweezers to place tiny lifting eyes on the engine deck.

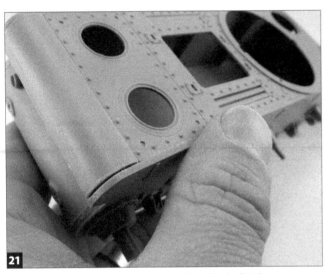

21 The engine intake cover is narrower than the hull sides.

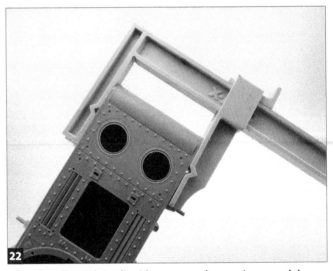

22 After liberally applying liquid cement to the gap, I snugged the hull sides against the intake cover with a lightweight plastic clamp.

sanding sprue attachment points. You want to be sure you don't remove more plastic than necessary and have to fill an uneven spot near the seam. It's better to work slowly here, removing a little at a time and checking your progress frequently, than it is to sand off too much.

Opening flashed-over holes. Many kits have optional parts. To model different versions of the same vehicle, the locators for those parts are often molded with the hole most of the way through with just a thin layer of plastic at the surface. Pay attention to the instructions, so these don't come as a surprise. The KV has several such holes on the hull sides. Round ones can be opened with a drill bit in a pin vise. For square openings like the KV has, I pushed the point of a fresh No. 11

blade through the plastic at the edges of the hole from the inside, **8**. Then, I cleaned up the holes from the outside with the knife and some sanding, **9**.

Dry-fitting—testing the fit of the parts before applying glue—is an important step that reveals problems with fit. It gives you a chance to correct those issues to ensure alignment and minimize gaps and filling. When I fit the KV's hull side, it was obvious something was interfering with the fit and causing unsightly gaps, **10**. The cause was obvious when I separated the parts. There were ejector-pin marks (circular marks left by the molding machine) on the back of the parts. Although they were recessed, there was a raised lip on several of them that prevented the parts from meeting. A few vigorous strokes with a sanding stick or sandpaper removed them, **11**.

Glues and mold seams. I used three types of glue when building the KV: Testors liquid cement, Tamiya extra thin liquid cement, and super glue. To join large parts with expansive gluing surfaces, I prefer using Testors liquid cement in the squeeze bottle with a metal tube applicator. Apply this cement to both surfaces and spread it with the metal tip, **12**. Then push the parts together, making sure they fit all the way around, **13**. Many parts exhibit raised mold seams, thin ridges of plastic left by the molding process, **14**. Most can be removed with simple sanding, **15**.

Pay attention to how parts are supposed to go together; the KV's rear hull didn't look like it fit when I dry-fit it because the lower lip protruded below the lower plate rather than being flush. Examination of the part and the subsequent

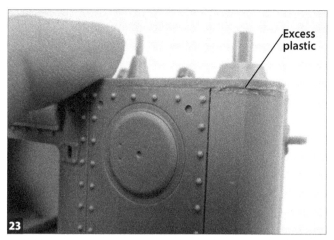

23

The liquid cement melted the plastic and filled the gap.

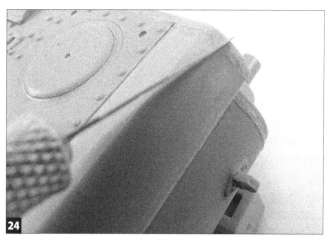

24

You can scrape excess plastic off a part with a hobby knife and then sand the seam smooth.

25

Sinkholes are shallow depression left in plastic surfaces as the plastic contracts after molding.

26

Squeeze a little Squadron white putty onto a disposable plastic lid.

27

Here's one time where it's good to have overfill. Always apply a little more putty than needed to fill the sinkhole.

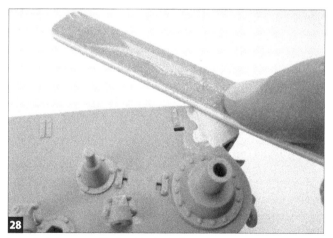

28

I sanded the putty flush with the hull, and when painted, it is impossible to tell that there was a sinkhole there.

construction diagrams showed that was the way it was supposed to be, **16**.

After applying the glue, I pushed the rear hull into place and discovered minor gaps along the edges. Applying pressure to the hull sides closed the gaps. There are commercial model clamps available,

but in this case, rubber bands worked just as well to keep the parts snug until the glue set, **17**. Before adding the small parts to the hull, I attached the upper hull sections.

Next, I attached the return-roller arms and other bits. Some needed cleanup

because of flash and ejector-pin marks, **18**. I attached these parts by holding them in position and touching a small brush of Tamiya liquid cement to the gap and letting capillary action draw it into the join, **19**. Tweezers are ideal for positioning small parts, **20**.

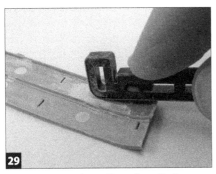

29 Filler putty and sanding also eliminate ejector-pin marks on the underside of the fenders.

30 Many armor kits feature two-part gun barrels. They require a little finesse to eliminate unsightly seams without sanding the barrel out of round.

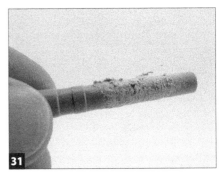

31 I applied putty to fill recessed rings on the barrel.

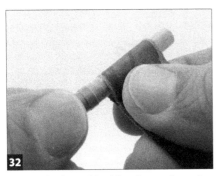

32 I spun the barrel inside a loop of sandpaper to smooth the putty and blend the halves.

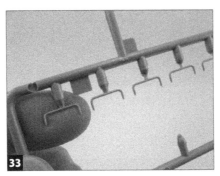

33 Delicate parts such as turret ladder rungs are best handled separately from other parts to avoid breakage.

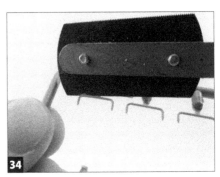

34 I cut through the sprue attachment point for one of the ladder rungs with a JLC razor saw.

35 After dipping a ladder rung in a puddle of super glue, I attached it to the turret.

36 To reinforce the tiny attachment point, I applied a little more super glue.

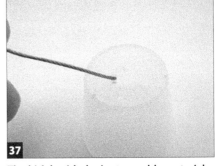

37 The kit's braided-wire tow cable material looks good but has a habit of fraying. Dip the ends in super glue to stop them from unraveling.

Filling gaps and holes. The last major part of the hull is the engine intake cover at the rear, but there was a large gap on one side, **21**. A simple clamp held the parts together while the glue set, **22**. I used slightly more liquid cement than necessary in the join, and the excess squeezed out during clamping, **23**. After it dried, I scraped it off with a hobby knife, **24**, and sanded it smooth.

On the KV, there were large sinkholes (depressions in the surface caused by shrinkage during molding) on each side of the rear hull, **25**. I filled them with modeling putty, in this case Squadron white, but there are several other brands with similar properties, **26**. Using a spatula, I globbed on more putty than necessary, partially because it shrinks a little as it dries, **27**. Putty takes several hours to dry all the way through, but once it is dry and smooth, it can be painted like plastic. I let it sit overnight and then sanded it flush with the surface, **28**.

I repeated this process to eliminate ejector-pin marks under the fenders, **29**. I finished the hull by adding the fenders and other details with liquid cement.

The turret. I turned my attention to the turret, the second major subassembly when building tanks. With the exception of a couple of problem areas, construction was simple. I removed prominent mold seams on the mantlet by scraping a hobby knife blade along the seam and smoothing the area with a sanding stick.

The gun barrel is molded in two parts with a separate muzzle, **30**. This can be a problem if the fit of the halves is not good. Heavy sanding on the barrel can leave the barrel out of round.

38

The KV is ready for painting. I left suspension and running gear off because I didn't think I could get paint behind and around them with a spray can.

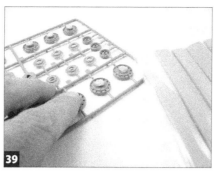

39

Mask the joining surfaces on the running gear with poster putty.

40

Unable to find Russian armor green in a spray can, I used Model Master dark green.

41

Spray cans produce a lot of paint at once. Start spraying off the model and make one continuous pass holding the can 6"–8" above the surface.

42

Spray misty for me: the first pass leaves the model looking pretty ugly, but it's better to build up the coverage with several light coats than one heavy, wet layer.

43

I applied a little glue to attach the road-wheel arms. There is a little play in the fit, and the slower-setting glue allows for adjustments.

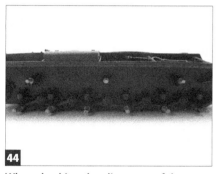

44

When checking the alignment of the suspension, place the hull on a flat surface to be sure that all of the arms are touching.

45

Heat and water produce corrosion, so I painted the exhausts Testors Model Master rust.

46

I painted the inside of the headlight Model Master chrome silver.

However, the KV's barrel fit well. To minimize sanding, I let Tamiya Thin Liquid Cement run down the joint and squeezed the parts together, forcing molten plastic to ooze from the gap. After the glue set, I shaved the bead of plastic with a fresh No. 11 blade and lightly sanded it. The barrel is divided into three segments by deep engraved rings that were not on the full-size tank, so I filled them in with putty, **31**. To prevent uneven sanding, I twisted the barrel against folded sandpaper, **32**.

Another unique feature of the turret is the three-rung ladders on either side that allowed the crew to reach the hatches on top of the turret. Each rung is molded scale thin and mounts to tiny depressions, **33**. When removing thin parts from the sprue, it's easy to damage them, so I used a fine razor saw and slowly cut through the attachments, **34**. Concerned that solvent-based model glue might melt and distort the thin plastic, I attached the rungs with super glue. Holding each rung with tweezers,

I dipped the ends in a small pool of super glue and positioned the rung on the model, **35**. To reinforce the joint, I applied a drop of super glue to each attachment point, **36**.

The kit includes copper-wire tow cables. Before cutting, I twisted the ends to eliminate any stray strands and dipped them in super glue to prevent the wire from unwinding, **37**. The wire was slightly too thick to fit the plastic cable loops so I bored the holes with a pin vise. Then the model was ready for painting, **38**.

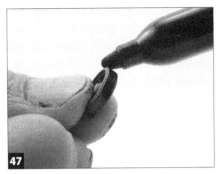

47

A black-ink permanent marker gives the tire on the KV's return rollers a nice rubbery sheen.

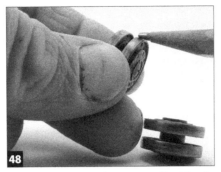

48

An easy way to produce a metallic shine is by drawing bare steel on the road-wheel rims with a soft pencil.

49

Vinyl tracks are an old standby for scale tank tracks. I melted the attachment pins with a heated screwdriver blade.

Pastel weathering
page 35

Airbrushing
page 18

Figure painting
page 82

Dry-brushing
page 25

Pinwash
page 30

Post-shading
page 62

Pigment weathering
page 69

Track painting
page 66

Groundwork
page 90

Spray-painting. Spray-painting produces smooth results that are difficult to achieve by brush-painting, especially on large surfaces. I left the wheels and suspension on the sprues for painting because spray cans aren't exactly built for precision. To keep paint off the joining surfaces, I masked them with poster putty, **39**. I used Testors Model Master enamel dark green (No. 1910), a close match to the color used on Soviet tanks in World War II, **40**.

Spray cans produce a high volume of paint so start spraying off the model, **41**. Keep the spray can about 6" above the surface and keep it moving continuously until you are past the model. Don't stop or reverse the spray on the model because too much paint will create runs. Also, don't aim for complete coverage on the first pass. Instead, the model should look speckled, **42**. It usually

takes two or three passes to produce a smooth, even finish.

I let the paint dry for 48 hours. Enamel paint takes time to cure all the way through, even though it may feel dry on top. Use the sniff test if you're not sure. If the model smells of paint fumes, the paint is still gassing out, and it may affect subsequent layers. I removed the masks from the suspension. To pick up any stray bits of poster putty, use a blob of putty to collect the stray pieces.

Final assembly. First, I added the running gear. Trumpeter keyed the road-wheel arms so alignment is fairly simple, **43**. It's a good idea to use slower-setting glue for the suspension, so you have time to make sure the arms line up and all of the wheels will be on the ground, **44**. Nothing ruins the illusion of heavy armor like wheels floating above the surface.

I started this project hoping to keep painting to a minimum, but there are a couple of things that needed it. I painted the exhaust on the engine deck Testors Model Master rust—heat and water equals corrosion, **45**. The inside of the headlight is Model Master enamel chrome silver, a beautifully smooth metallic with a shine that's perfect for small details and light, **46**. I attached the lens with Testors Clear Parts Cement.

KV return rollers have a thin tire. I carefully drew on the rubber with a black permanent-ink marker, **47**. For the exposed metal rims on the road wheels, I used a soft lead pencil, **48**.

Finally, I added the vinyl tracks, carefully melting the ends with the heated tip of a screwdriver, **49**. But that's not the end of the story.... After the initial build, I revisited the KV using some of the other techniques from this book, and put it on a display base.

Learning about
TOOLS

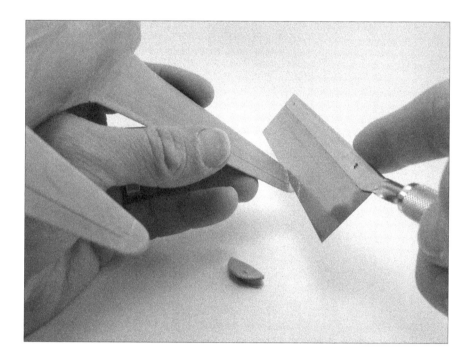

Skills

- Selecting knives and blades
- Sanding and filing
- Storing tools

The basic tools that modelers use are listed here by their purpose. This list is by no means exhaustive; I'm constantly finding new bits and pieces, and it seems like there are always new items on the market designed to make your life easier. My aim is to cover the basics—the items you'll use almost every session—as well as a few of the most useful specialized tools.

1 Useful knives include those with retractable blades (top) and metal-handle knives that allow you to use various blade shapes.

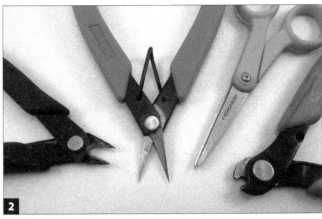

2 Cutting tools that modelers should have are, from left, sprue cutters, a shears for cutting thin brass or steel, a scissors for trimming decals, and a wire shears.

3 Modelers use sandpaper of various grades, specialized sanders, and foam core sanding sticks, which come in grades from coarse to extra fine.

4 For handling parts, you should have, clockwise from bottom, long pointed, curved-head, flat-head, and reverse tweezers. You should also have a smooth-jawed pliers and a needlenose pair.

Knives. I use several hobby knives, and there is always one out while I'm working. Hobby knives are available in various styles, and the most useful ones are the metal handles that contain interchangeable blades made by X-Acto, Excel, and others. They are generally inexpensive, and the variety of blades, as well as the ease of changing them, makes them especially versatile, **1**. Among the blade shapes, I find that I use the No. 11 with its long, straight cutting edge and sharp point 95 percent of the time. I also keep a variety pack with chisel and curved blades handy.

Retractable-blade knives are also useful, especially for big jobs. Some modelers prefer scalpels as their fine, sharp, interchangeable blades. And sometimes nothing will do but a single-edged razor blade. Whatever kind of knife you use, be sure to keep fresh blades on hand. The finely honed edges on most blades are quickly dulled and can damage the parts or materials you are working with.

Snips, shears, and scissors. After the hobby knife, the best tool you can own is a good pair of sprue cutters, **2**. Also known as side cutters, its blades differ from wire cutters by having one side of the blades perpendicular to the cutting plane. The result is a precise cut close to the surface of a part.

Similar tools with very fine points are sold for working with photoetched metal, and there are even tools similar to tin shears that will cut through the thin brass or steel used in photoetched-metal details.

I also like to have a dedicated pair of scissors for trimming decals. Wire shears, designed to cut wire squarely, rather than leaving tapered, jagged ends, are great when scratchbuilding.

Sanders and files. As a kid, the first sanding tool I used on models was an emery board given to me by my mother. Now, there are dozens of sanders and files available to modelers, **3**. I like using foam core sanding sticks for cleaning up most parts. They come in a variety of grades, and the foam core has some give that makes it easy to avoid sanding too hard and producing flat spots. They also come in several shapes for getting into tight spots.

Sandpaper is a big part of my toolbox too. In addition to the stuff sold to modelers, check out the finer grades sold at hardware and home improvement stores. Grits range from 180 to 2000. Specialized sanders are also available. They use a variety of shapes and materials, so you shouldn't have any trouble finding what you need, no matter the shape or size of the object or area to be sanded.

Metal files may be too rough for most plastic applications, but I recommend getting a set of riffler files. They come in different shapes and are a handy addition for filing tight spots or odd shapes.

Tweezers and pliers. Unless you have itsy-bitsy fingers, you'll need tweezers to handle small parts, **4**. There are several types sold. I recommend having a long, pointed pair for getting small parts into tight spots, a curved-head pair for tight angles, and a flat-head set for handling decals. A reverse pair can also be useful.

I keep two sets of pliers handy, a standard pair—for opening stubborn bottles—and a needlenose pair. The needle-nose pair can handle small parts and serve as a bending tool for wire and photoetched metal. If you plan on folding a lot of parts, consider buying a smooth-jawed pair.

Saws. Unlike knives, which cut by forcing material apart, saws gradually remove material at the cut. This makes them great for removing delicate parts as well as for making straight cuts when trimming items. Hobby saws come in a bunch of sizes and blade shapes, **5**.

For making precise straight cuts in styrene, resin, and metal, I use a large-bladed saw that came with a miter box. In addition, I have a small, wooden-handled saw with a double-sided blade about the size of a razor. It's perfect for trimming parts and re-scribing damaged panel lines. There are even saw blades that fit hobby-knife handles.

Pin vise. A pin vise and a set of mini-drill bits are essential, **6**. You can open shallow holes with the point of a No. 11 blade, but a pin vise will make your life easier.

Tape. We'll look at masking in more detail in other chapters, but I use several different kinds of tape. I especially like Tamiya's thin yellow paper tape for masking, but I keep a roll of low-tack blue painter's tape on hand for masking large areas. Tape can also be used to hold parts in position while glue dries.

Supports and third hands. Many times when building or painting you'll need something to hold the part or model you

5 A large-bladed saw is great for making straight cuts, and one with a double-sided blade is perfect for trimming parts.

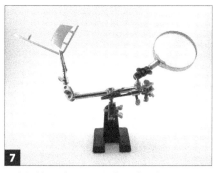

7 A third hand comes in handy when you have to glue or paint small parts.

are working on, either because you need both hands or you risk knocking parts off if you set the model down. I keep some small cardboard boxes around for that, but a third hand is also a great addition to the workbench, **7**.

For painting, something as simple as a wire coat hanger can serve as a paint stand, but there are also commercial paint stands and turntables.

Household items. A variety of common items found around the house can be used as helpful modeling tools. While you're at the grocery store, pick up some toothpicks. The round ones make good glue applicators and can even paint dots. Flat toothpicks can be used to stir paint and apply putty. Cotton pads are useful for cleaning tools and models. Rubber bands and twist ties make great adjustable clamps.

Don't overlook containers and lids that might otherwise be thrown out. Jars make good brush cleaners and plastic coffee-can lids and old gift cards are great disposable glue and paint palettes. I use yogurt cups to mix paint and thinner in for airbrushing.

Motor tool. A rotary motor tool, such as those made by Dremel, can make quick work of some modeling jobs, **8**. Look for a variable-speed model. The most useful bits are cut-off wheels, sanding drums,

6 For opening holes and drilling new ones, a pin vise is a must.

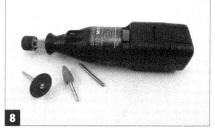

8 With many bits available, a variable-speed rotary motor tool can handle a wide range of modeling jobs. Cut-off wheels, sanding drums, and grinding bits are most useful.

and grinding bits. Motor tools work quickly, and it's easy to make mistakes, so be careful when using one. Also, always wear eye protection.

Safety supplies. Latex gloves protect your skin from potential irritants such as paint and thinner when you are spray-painting or airbrushing. Also look for a good dual-cartridge respirator to use when painting or sanding to protect your lungs. Keep a few bandages on hand for the inevitable knife slips—fingers bleed a lot, and blood doesn't improve paint jobs.

A place to work. While most modelers dream of having a room dedicated to their hobby, many masterpieces have been built in less glamorous digs, including on coffee tables and in closets.

Magnificent or modest, the chief requirements of any work space are good lighting, such as a dedicated lamp—it really helps when you can see what you are doing—and ventilation. I use a small fan to keep glue and paint fumes from collecting. Remember, if you can smell it, you're breathing it.

If you don't have access to drawers and shelves to store supplies, consider using a tackle box or parts organizer to keep your tools and finishing supplies squared away until your next building session.

3

Brushing up on AIRBRUSHING

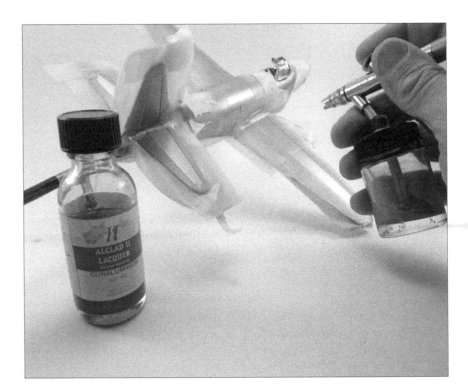

Skills

- Learning techniques
- Blending
- Mixing paint
- Troubleshooting

There are few skills more likely to improve your modeling than airbrushing. It transforms painting from uneven brush strokes or difficult-to-control spray cans to applying precise even finishes and allowing for blending and soft transitions. There have been many books written about airbrushing, and modeling magazines routinely cover the subject. What follows is a brief introduction to the tools, how to use them, and how to maintain them.

1

The core of any airbrush is the nozzle and needle. They may change size depending on the brush, but airflow over and through them produces the spray that moves paint to the model.

What is an airbrush? Designs differ, but in simple terms, an airbrush compresses air and pushes it through a narrow nozzle where it atomizes paint and blows it out in a controllable pattern, **1**. Think about it as a miniaturized, precision version of the paint sprayers used for houses and cars. Airbrushes are used in many professions and hobbies, and they are the perfect tool for applying paint to scale models.

Single- versus double-action. Airbrush designs differ, but they can be divided into two basic categories: single-action and double-action. Airbrush types can affect the way paint is applied, their ease of use, and cleaning properties.

In a single-action brush, the trigger controls only air flow, and it's usually either on or off, **2**. Paint flow is preset by adjusting either the nozzle or the needle. This makes them easy to use, especially for beginners, because there's only one thing to consider while spraying and a lot less chance of applying too much paint. On the other hand, single-action brushes tend to be less versatile because adjusting the paint flow is generally done while the brush is not in use.

On a double-action airbrush, the trigger controls air flow and paint volume, **3**. Generally, the air pressure is controlled by depressing the trigger. Pulling back on the trigger moves the needle within the nozzle, which allows more paint through and results in a wider pattern. Skilled painters can manipulate double-action brushes to easily create interesting effects. But the versatility of double-action brushes makes them harder to use as there are more variables to master.

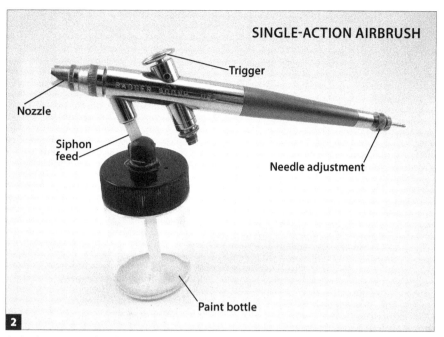

SINGLE-ACTION AIRBRUSH

Trigger

Nozzle

Siphon feed

Needle adjustment

Paint bottle

2

A single-action airbrush is easy to use, as the trigger controls only air flow, but one can also be less versatile.

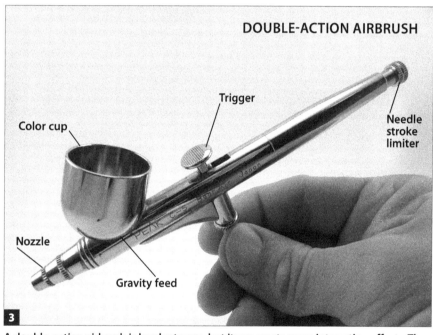

DOUBLE-ACTION AIRBRUSH

Trigger

Color cup

Needle stroke limiter

Nozzle

Gravity feed

3

A double-action airbrush is harder to use, but it can create more interesting effects. The trigger controls air flow as well as paint volume.

External versus internal mix. An airbrush can mix paint and air in two ways, either externally or internally. External brushes are usually less expensive than internal brushes, but they tend to produce a wider, harder-to-control spray pattern. I find internal mix brushes easier to use and control, but I know many talented builders who achieve terrific results with external-mix brushes.

Bottles, color cups, and gravity feed. Airbrushes hold paint either in a bottle that attaches to the brush, usually from underneath, or in an open-top color cup. Bottles hold more paint and can be closed, a handy way to prevent unfortunate spills or splashes. Most color cups mount on top of the brush. They hold less paint, but because gravity helps move paint into the body of the brush as opposed to air pressure in a bottle-fed

4 A common air supply is canned propellant.

5 Compressors come in many shapes and sizes. This Iwata single-piston model features a built-in regulator and water trap.

6 A regulator allows you to better control the pressure.

7 An in-line water trap stops moisture problems.

8 A compressed-air tank is a quiet source of power.

9 A gas cylinder is another air source.

brush, you don't have to use as high a pressure to spray. That means you can achieve subtle effects more easily.

Air supply. Most airbrush starter sets come with a can of propellant and those will work fine for basic finishes, **4**. When using canned propellant, stand the can in warm water. The heat will help the can maintain pressure. The disadvantages of using propellant are the expense of constantly having to replace the cans and the difficulty of controlling the pressure.

Most modelers end up using a compressor once they are comfortable with airbrushing, and like the airbrush, they can be an important investment in your hobby, **5**. Many manufacturers sell different styles. I recommend a diaphragm or piston-powered unit that can maintain a steady pressure of at least 22 psi. A unit with a storage tank is even better. That said, even small, tabletop compressors will move paint through a brush. Some compressors come with built-in regulators, **6**. If you get one that doesn't, consider purchasing one because it'll give you control over one of the variables of airbrushing—pressure.

Pick up a moisture trap while you're at it. As air is compressed, any moisture present condenses. If water from the air line hits the fresh paint on the model, the color may be ruined. A moisture trap will stop drops of water from reaching the brush, **7**.

One more thing to consider is noise. Compressors are, as a rule, noisy. If you live alone miles from your nearest neighbor, you can get away the biggest, loudest machine you can find. If you share a house with others, or live in an apartment, your friends and neighbors will thank you for choosing a quiet alternative.

A third option for powering your brush is compressed air or gas. Look for portable air tanks at hardware and home improvement stores, **8**. They are reasonably inexpensive—around $35—and when you lose pressure, you can top it off at a gas station. The gauge on the tank shows how much air is left in the tank; you'll need an in-line regulator/moisture trap to control pressure.

You can also use an industrial gas cylinder, filled with air, nitrogen, or carbon dioxide, **9**. These are available from specialized outlets—restaurant or bar supply stores for CO_2 and welding shops for nitrogen—and come in several sizes. You won't need a moisture trap if you're using nitrogen or CO_2 but you'll need a regulator. Portable air tanks and gas cylinders have a big advantage—they are silent.

Where to airbrush? Airbrushing, by definition, makes paint airborne and easily inhaled, which is unhealthy. Personally, I need to hang on to all of my remaining brain cells, so it's important to airbrush where there is good ventilation—outdoors or in a garage with the door open—rather than in an enclosed space. (Some paint fumes are even flammable, so it's really a bad idea to let them build up in a room or basement containing a gas-fired heater or stove.)

The best option is a spray booth. Not only will the fan pull paint fumes and particles out of the room, but it will contain stray paint and help avoid accidental redecoration. Many booths are available commercially, and magazines such as *FineScale Modeler* occasionally publish articles showing how to build your own.

Whether you build or buy a booth, the features to keep in mind are size, filter type, fan size and type, and light-

ing. Model tanks and cars are a lot easier to maneuver in tight spaces such as a spray booth than, say, a 1/48 scale B-17 is. Determine if replacement filters are commonly available or hard to find. Make sure the fan is strong enough to pull paint quickly out of the booth. Supply adequate lighting. You can't airbrush well if you can't see where the paint is going. Also, be sure you can run the vent outdoors through a window or a hole similar to a dryer vent.

A variety of variables. If there is a constant in airbrushing, it's that there are variables. Learning to control those variables and use them is the key to mastering the airbrush. These variables, in no particular order, are air pressure, paint viscosity, paint volume, and distance to the surface. Airbrushing is about numbers. I know—no one told you there'd be math. Don't worry. The numbers aren't complicated, but they're a way of communicating the variables.

Air pressure, measured in pounds per square inch (psi), is controlled by the regulator on the air supply and can be fine-tuned using the trigger on double-action airbrushes. The higher the pressure, the faster paint moves through the brush. I've found that external-mix brushes need more pressure than internal-mix ones. And siphon-feed brushes need a little more than gravity-feed brushes to achieve similar results. While not set in stone, I usually use higher pressure for general coverage and lower pressure for detail work and fine lines.

Paint viscosity is about paint's relative thinness and the ease with which it flows through the brush. Paint needs to be thinner for airbrushing than it does for brush-painting, so paint thinner needs to be added. Most paint manufac-

10 When it's ready to airbrush, paint should run smoothly and easily down the side of the container.

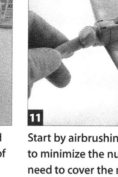
11 Start by airbrushing corners and recesses to minimize the number of passes you need to cover the model and reduce runs.

12 For general painting, hold the brush 4"–5" off the model and keep it moving. Always start and finish painting off the model.

13 Excessive paint (center) might be a problem but don't rub it off while the paint is wet—it'll smear and look worse.

14 Sometimes all you need is patience. Several hours after I sprayed on too much paint, the problem became invisible.

15 The first stage of airbrush cleaning is blowing clean thinner through it to flush any paint residue from the system.

turers have recommended thinners and thinning ratios printed on the bottles, although you may need a magnifier to read it. That is a good starting point. Aim for paint that is about as thick as 2 percent milk. Another way to measure is by touching a toothpick with paint on an end against the side of the paint-mixing container: if it runs down evenly, you're in the ballpark, **10**.

Paint volume refers to the amount of paint flowing past the nozzle onto the surface of the model. You control it by moving the needle relative to the nozzle—the farther back, the larger the opening and the more paint being expelled. On single-action airbrushes, the needle is moved manually before spraying; the trigger pull adjusts it on double-action brushes.

Distance to the surface may seem obvious, but it can be hard to perfect. There's a fine line between just right and being too close or too far away. When I started airbrushing, I was gun shy and, fearing paint runs, held the brush almost 12" away. Ideally, hold the brush 4"–5" away and adjust the distance as necessary for various effects.

Basic technique. After thinning the paint and connecting the brush to your air supply, you're ready to paint. The most important thing to remember is to keep the airbrush a consistent distance, 4"–5" away, and perpendicular to the surface. Keep the brush moving but try not to reverse direction to prevent excess paint covering the model. As when spray-painting, always start and finish spraying off the model.

For example, when airbrushing an airplane, I start by painting corners and recesses, such as wing roots and weld seams, with the nozzle set to a narrower pattern, **11**. This ensures good coverage while minimizing the chances of runs and drips caused by too much paint. When satisfied that the hard-to-reach areas are painted, I set the brush to a wider spray pattern and cover broad areas of the wings and fuselage, **12**. You don't want complete coverage on the first pass. Build up the paint in several light coats.

There's a fine line between just the right amount and too much paint. If you think you've gone too far, step back and wait. Don't be tempted to wipe off runs or excess paint while painting, **13**. Instead, leave the model alone to dry. You might

be surprised how well some paints, especially acrylics, level during drying, **14**.

Additional tips. For fine lines or small patches like Luftwaffe World War II mottling, use thinner paint and lower pressure and keep the airbrush perpendicular to the surface to limit overspray. You can hold the tip of the brush very close to the surface, but lower the pressure to prevent flooding the surface with paint.

If airbrushing against masks, keep the brush perpendicular to the edge and make as few passes as possible at a mask's edge to prevent a ridge of paint forming.

If you are applying a freehand camouflage, outline each area with a fine line, then fill in the area with paint. You can adjust the feather of the edge by changing the angle of the brush relative to the surface. Spraying straight down will give an average softness to the edge. Holding the brush at 45 degrees and spraying toward the center of the area being painted will sharpen the line considerably.

Cleanup. The key to a good finish is keeping the airbrush clean, so it's important to clean it after each painting session.

BETTER BRUSH-PAINTING

Most modelers get comfortable using an airbrush, but it's important to not forget the humble paintbrush. Good brushing will make painting details like wheels, cockpits, and figures easy and produce good-looking models.

Let's talk brushes. It's easy to get overwhelmed by the choices of brush size and shape as well as the type of bristle. Bristle selection is more a matter of taste, but I favor fine, soft bristles, such as sable, for detail work. These brushes tend to be more expensive, but the investment is worth it in better finishes. I also prefer longer handles for better control.

Cleaning is all about care and proper storage. As a kid, I put just-used paintbrushes into a coffee can full of dirty turpentine. There they would sit until I needed them again. In no time, the bristles were bent and broken, and it was almost impossible to paint an even line. Now, I own several brushes that have put in stellar service for years. Store your brushes with the bristles pointing up. A glass or cup is perfect. Some fine brushes include a protective plastic sleeve—use it. You can protect your other brushes by storing them in cut-down drinking straws or coffee stirrers.

Fine-pointed, round brushes are great for painting details and applying pinwashes.

Larger rounds are great for covering larger areas, as well as transferring or mixing paint.

Flat brushes give you an edge: they make it easy to create sharp demarcation lines and lay down a smooth layer of paint.

Using a palette minimizes the time a bottle is open. Acrylic paint can develop a skin over its surface, and, over time, affect its quality.

Every time you tip the brush in the paint, drag it across an edge to remove excess paint.

Stir the paint with a toothpick or piece of sprue, making sure all the solids that may have collected at the bottom get mixed.

Then, transfer a small amount of paint to a well in the palette with an eyedropper. Place a little thinner in another well.

Dip the brush into thinner before starting and wipe it on a paper towel. Moistening the bristles helps paint flow and prevents it from drying in the brush.

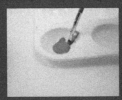

Now dip the brush into the paint. Do not completely immerse the bristles. Capillary action will draw the paint into the brush.

Place the brush onto the surface and draw it along, generally keeping to the direction of surface detail or panel lines.

Keep strokes going in one direction and paint back to the area most recently painted without going over the same area too many times. This minimizes brush strokes, and some paints can be pulled up by the brush if they have started to dry.

Adding thinner can help paint flow. This can mean easy, clean edges by letting thin paint run around demarcation lines, such as between a tire and wheel, and then filling in the rest with normal paint.

Keep a jar of thinner handy while painting. Place the brush so the bristles are submerged but not against the bottom and gently roll them against the side. You should be able to see the paint floating out.

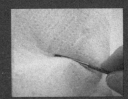

Draw the brush through a folded paper towel while squeezing gently. You can also massage a 2-in-1 shampoo and conditioner into the bristles and rinse it out. This will remove paint and thinner residue while rejuvenating the hairs.

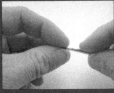

Finally, shape the head with your fingertips.

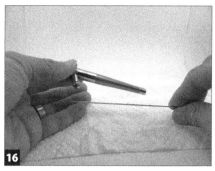

16 Be careful when removing the needle as it's easily damaged. Fortunately, needles are easily replaced through a well-stocked hobby store or from the manufacturer.

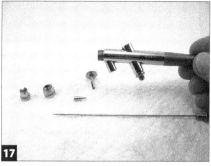

17 Next comes the nozzle, usually trapped at the front of the brush. The small item is delicate, and any crimps or splits in the metal will cause paint to splatter.

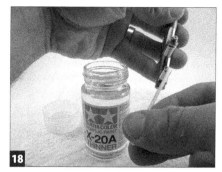

18 Cotton swabs tipped in thinner will get into most parts of the brush. Use pipe cleaners to clean small holes and other tight spaces.

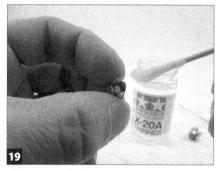

19 Clean around the nozzle to prevent paint from building up and affecting paint flow.

20 Drag the needle through a paper towel damp with thinner to keep it smooth.

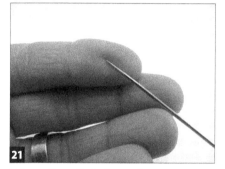

21 Using a fingertip is the perfect way to check for needle problems.

First, spray clean thinner through the brush at high pressure to get rid of as much paint as possible, **15**. Hold your finger over the nozzle as you depress the trigger to blow thinner back through the nozzle's paint channels and blow any paint out.

Next, remove the needle, **16**. Be very careful not to bend the tip. Then remove the front end and carefully take out the delicate nozzle, **17**. Using thinner on cotton swabs or pipe cleaners, scrub paint from inside and outside of the brush, **18** and **19**.

Pull the needle through a paper towel or cotton rag damp with thinner. Don't push it or you risk bending the point, **20**. Check the point by dragging the needle across your fingertip while turning it, **21**. If you feel it catch, then the tip is bent, and it will affect the paint pattern. If it's minor, you can drag the tip across a nail buffer to reshape it.

Assemble the brush and then spray out a little more thinner to be sure it's clean.

If you are concerned about paint residue in the brush, you can soak the metal parts, but be sure to remove any rubber seals or gaskets because the thinner will destroy them. Also, ammonia-based cleaners, such as Windex, work well to clean up after acrylics, but ammonia will etch brass

so don't soak any parts in it. Lacquer thinner dissolves acrylics and enamels, so it can be a good general cleaner.

Troubleshooting. There are a few things that can go wrong when airbrushing, and most are caused by a problem with one of the variables mentioned earlier.

An **orange peel**, or grainy finish, means that either the paint is too thick and not settling properly (mix in a little more thinner) or the brush is too far away from the surface and the paint is drying before it lands or has the chance to level itself (move the brush closer). Ideally, paint should look wet as it lands. If you are spraying a flat color, it should look wet for a few seconds after hitting the surface.

Runs are a sign that either the paint is too thin (add more paint to the mix) or the brush is staying too long in one place (keep the brush moving). Don't try to wipe runs off the model; instead, wait until the paint dries and sand it down and respray if necessary.

Thin spots, especially where the paint appears to be pulling away from high spots or corners, indicate that the paint is too thin. To correct, you can add more paint, a few drops at a time, until the mix looks right.

Fisheyes (funny name, serious problem) occur when oil, grease, or other contaminants on the surface interfere with paint adhesion. Prevention is the best cure so clean the model with alcohol or Testors Plastic Prep before spraying. Minor fisheyes may be corrected by sanding after the paint dries and repainting, but major ones will require you to strip the model and start again.

Wrinkling or cracking is a symptom of paint incompatibility, or it occurs if the underlying layer is not completely dry when the following layer has been applied. The general rule is to use the same type of paint on a project. You should be able to apply enamels and acrylics over lacquers but not lacquer over any other kind. And don't spray acrylics over enamels. Also, make sure each layer is dry before applying the next. Use the sniff test: if you can smell paint, there is still gas coming out of it, and it's not completely cured.

Practice, practice, practice. The best way to learn airbrushing is by doing it. It may seem daunting at first, but you'll become familiar with the brush and how it works. And use it—a lot. Build a few models to try different techniques. Once you get the hang of it, I guarantee that you'll never look back.

4

Modeling AIRCRAFT

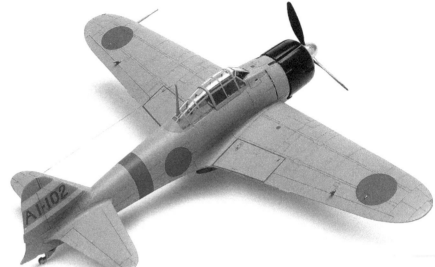

Skills

- Basic aircraft modeling
- Repairing lost panel lines
- Seam filling
- Working with clear parts
- Masking canopies
- Decaling
- Applying washes

Mitsubishi A6M2b ZERO FIGHTER TYPE 21 'PEARL HARBOR'

Hasegawa's 1/48 scale A6M2 Zero is a good example of a modern aircraft kit. It has fine, recessed panel lines, a detailed cockpit and engines, and colorful decals. Let's jump right in.

Aircraft models, unlike armor, always have interior detail, usually cockpits and engines that must be painted and built before gluing the fuselage together, **1**. There is almost always a paint key, **2**, to help you decode the color callouts shown in the exploded view diagrams, **3**. I started by brush-painting the cockpit and engine parts with Tamiya acrylics while they were attached to the sprue, **4**. The parts tree works as a handle, which makes painting easier. Some of the small, round parts had mold seams that I removed with a hobby knife before painting, **5**.

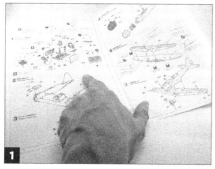

1 Aircraft models almost always start with the cockpit or interior. Once the fuselage is closed, those areas are off limits.

2 Before getting too deep into the project, I consulted the kit's paint chart for color information.

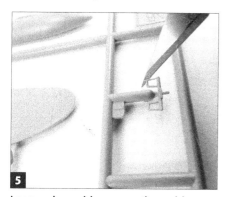

3 Instruction have color callouts, sometimes with names and, as with the Hasegawa Zero, sometimes just as numbers.

4 I painted the kit's engine Tamiya metallic gray, my interpretation of the Mr. Hobby steel called for by the instructions.

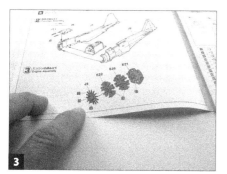

5 I scraped a mold seam on the rudder pedals.

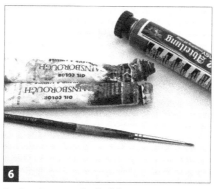

6 Recipe for a wash: dark brown or black artist's oil, a fine brush, and a thinner such as Turpenoid.

MITSUBISHI A6M ZERO

Fast and maneuverable, the Mitsubishi A6M outperformed every Allied fighter it faced in the opening months of World War II. Best known as the Zero, the aircraft is also referred to as the Reisen or Zeke. More Zeros were produced than any other Japanese aircraft, and the airplane became a symbol of Japan's power. When it debuted in 1939, the

A Zero takes off from the Japanese carrier *Akagi* to attack Pearl Harbor on December 7, 1941. *U.S. National Archives photo*

A6M1 was unsurpassed in maneuverability, range, armaments, and speed (491 kilometers per hour). The installation of a more powerful engine and subsequent redesign (A6M2) boosted its top speed to more than 533 kph, and a legend was born.

Stories of the fighter's success in China in 1940 and against American and Commonwealth fighters after Pearl Harbor gave it an air of invincibility that wasn't broken until the Allies captured and evaluated an intact aircraft. The revealed shortcomings and the appearance of new powerful, well-armed, and well-protected Allied fighters, such as the Hellcat, turned the tables. Despite updates and new engines, the Zero never regained its preeminent position, eventually being relegated to the role of Kamikaze attacker.

Using a wash. Once the details were painted and while the parts were still unassembled, I applied a wash to highlight the detail. Because the base is acrylic, I used artist's oils thinned with Turpenoid, **6**. The type of wash you use depends on the kind of paint the model is painted with: generally, you should use enamel or oil washes over acrylics and acrylic washes over enamels or lacquers.

After squeezing out a little raw umber oil paint, I added a little Turpenoid to a well in the palette. (I prefer dark brown to black for washes because it looks more

natural.) Then, using a soft, round brush, I mixed just a little paint into a pool of thinner in a third palette well, **7**. It's better to work slowly up to the color density you want, and it doesn't take a lot of paint to darken the thinner. A good measure of the tone of the wash is to squeeze the excess from the brush against the side of the well, **8**.

The secret of a wash is to let the thin paint naturally collect in recesses and along edges. I ran the brush over each of the parts until I was sure it was completely coated, **9**. The shade usually gets slightly

lighter as it dries, but the effect is subtle shadow detail, **10**. One of the best things about using artist's oil washes over acrylics is that they can be easily changed if you don't like the effect. On the Zero's floor, the paint left a slight ring at high tide, **11**. I applied a little clear thinner, and it smoothed out the finish, **12**.

Dry-brushing. To further highlight the cockpit, dry-brushing the raised detail works well. First, mix the base paint with white about 50:50, **13**. Dip an old flat brush in the paint and rub the bristles across a

7 I added a little raw umber artist's oil paint to a palette. There is Turpenoid in the well at the right.

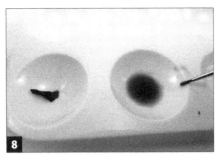

8 I checked the density of the wash by seeing how dark it is running down the side of the palette.

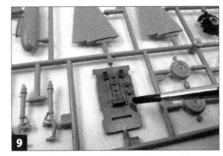

9 It doesn't take much to apply a wash. Lightly move the brush over the surface until it is completely wet.

10 As the wash collects in corners of the cockpit walls, it creates natural shadows.

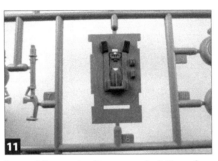

11 I wasn't happy to discover a dark line of wash on the cockpit floor…

12 …but a little clear thinner dissolved the line and repaired the damage.

13 I lightened Tamiya cockpit green with white in preparation for dry-brushing the cockpit.

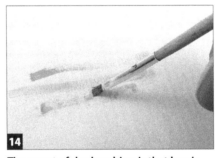

14 The secret of dry-brushing is that less is more. I wiped off most of the paint on a paper towel.

15 Lightly pass the almost-paintless brush over the cockpit's raised details…

paper towel until no paint comes off, **14**. Then stroke the brush lightly across the surface of the part, **15**. It should leave a little of the lighter shade on edges and ridges, **16**.

Cockpit and fuselage. After adding the decal instrument faces and painting details, **17**, scrape paint from the attachment points on the cockpit parts, **18**. Assemble the cockpit parts, **19**, and then check its fit against the fuselage halves, **20**. Hold the fuselage halves together and apply slow-setting liquid cement to the seam with a fine brush, **21**. Squeeze the halves together so molten plastic oozes from the gap, **22**. Plastic clamps sold for modeling can help hold the parts together as the glue sets, **23**. After scraping excess plastic from the seams with a

hobby knife, smooth the joins with sandpaper. To avoid damage to surrounding detail, run strips of masking tape along each side of the seam, **24**.

Wings. Some kits have details that need to be removed for the version you want to build. On the Hasegawa Zero, this includes trim tabs and actuators on the wings. Use sprue cutters to remove most of the raised actuators and then shave the rest with a sharp hobby knife, **25**. Be careful not to shave too much of the plastic or gouge into the surface. Follow up with sanding sticks or sandpaper, **26**.

Super glue is the perfect filler for the fine recessed lines outlining the trim tabs. Apply the glue to the lines with the bent tip of a toothpick, **27**. Follow

up with accelerator applied just above the glue and allow it to flow over the gap, **28**. It'll set the glue instantly, and then you just wipe the excess accelerator from the surface with a paper towel. Sand the gap within a few minutes of applying the accelerator; if it is left too long, the super glue will set harder than the plastic and be hard to sand, **29**. Run the tip of a toothpick along the engraved panel lines to remove sanding residue, **30**.

After opening holes in the wings for mass balances and the aileron actuator, glue the upper wing halves to the one-piece lower wing and carefully sand the leading edges, **31**. Rock the sanding stick over the curve of the leading edge to avoid flat spots.

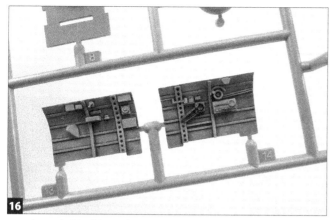

16

...to leave behind just a little paint on corners and ridges.

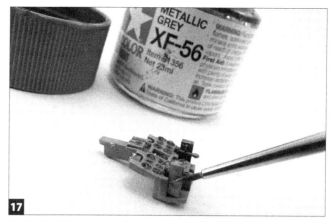

17

Apply decal instrument faces and paint fine details such as the machine-gun breeches.

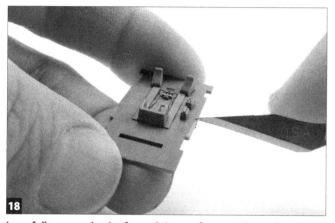

18

I carefully scraped paint from gluing surfaces on the cockpit parts.

19

The cockpit components are laid out and ready to assemble.

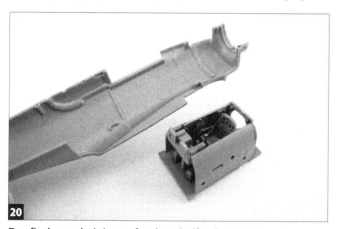

20

Dry-fit the cockpit into a fuselage half to be sure there's no question about its position.

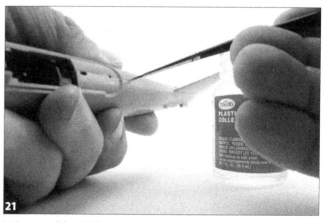

21

Using an old paintbrush, apply Testors liquid cement to the fuselage. The slow-setting glue allows time to get the fit right.

Aligning flying surfaces. I attached the Zero's horizontal stabilizers and then the wings. Check the instructions and your references to ensure you get them positioned correctly. Nothing ruins the appearance of an airplane like uneven wings or tail plane, so it's important to align them. The A6M2's horizontal stabs should be perpendicular to the vertical tail. After applying liquid cement to the

join, I held the fuselage on its side and let gravity aid alignment, **32**.

I ran into a couple of minor snags when I attached the wing; there were large gaps on the top at the wing root, **33**, and small steps at the nose and belly. The solution for the former was elegantly simple. First, I glued the wing to the fuse-lage at the nose and rear but not at the wing root. The next day, I stretched tape

from wingtip to wingtip, running it under the tips and across the body to pull the wings up against the fuselage, **34**. Then I ran liquid cement into the join and set it aside to dry overnight. I was left with a very little gap to fill, and it corrected the model's dihedral.

To fix the steps, I blended the step at the rear with Squadron putty and sanding, **35**.

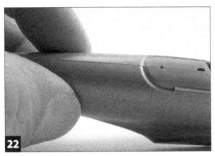

22 A bead of molten plastic oozes from the fuselage seam as I squeeze the halves together.

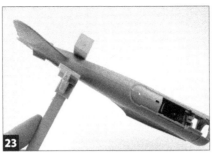

23 To be sure the fuselage stays together as the glue sets, I secured it with an X-Acto plastic clamp.

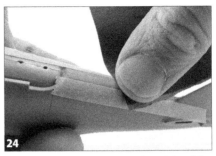

24 Strips of masking tape on either side of the seam protect the fuselage from damage while I clean up the join.

25 Shave an unneeded tab actuator, a detail seen on later Zeros, from the lower wing.

26 A sanding stick removes the last remnants of the actuator. Sand in small circles to prevent damage to other areas.

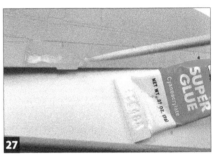

27 Fill in the unneeded trim tab by applying thin super glue to the engraved outline.

28 A little accelerator goes a long way. Apply the kicker uphill from the super glue and let it flow down.

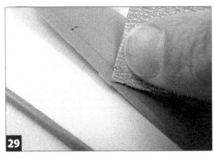

29 Immediately after the glue sets, sand it flush with the surface.

30 I removed sanding and glue residue from panel lines with a toothpick to avoid scratching the plastic.

Canopy. Before starting on the clear parts, paint the deck behind the cockpit opening with the indicated cockpit color and the area in front flat black, **36**. Once you attach the canopy, you won't be able to reach these areas. Mask the canopy (see sidebar on page 44) and then attach its three parts—windscreen, fixed rear section, and sliding section—in that order with Testors Clear Parts Cement, **37**. I wanted the option to pose the canopy open, so I tacked the center part with four small dots of glue.

Painting prep. If you plan to paint with acrylics, it's important that the surface be clean and free of any oils such as a mold-release agent or skin oil. I recommend applying Testors Surface Prep with a cotton ball or pad, **38**. Rub surface prep over the entire model and let it air dry. The surface prep also helps with static electricity, which can attract dust and hair to your model and ruin the finish. To avoid marring fresh paint with fingerprints and to minimize awkward shuffling during painting, attach a handle to the model, **39**.

Airbrushing acrylics. Most paints need to be thinned for airbrushing, although many acrylics need less than enamels. I used Tamiya acrylics on my Zero, paints that generally need to be mixed with more than average amounts of thinner to spray cleanly. Using eyedroppers, I transferred equal amounts of paint and Tamiya thinner to a Badger 200 siphon

bottle. Tamiya's thinner appears to have a little acrylic paint retarder mixed in, so the paint doesn't dry as quickly as other acrylics. This gives it more of a chance to level and produce a smooth finish. Stir the paint rather than shaking it; shaking can introduce bubbles that may end up on your model, **40**. When you have the consistency you like, about the same as 2 percent milk, you're ready to paint.

First things first. I painted the canopy frame Tamiya cockpit green, **41**. It'll be covered by the body color later, but the inside will match the rest of the cockpit. While waiting for the frame to dry, I airbrushed the engine cowl semigloss black, **42**. Keep the airbrush moving and the cowl turning to avoid paint buildup and

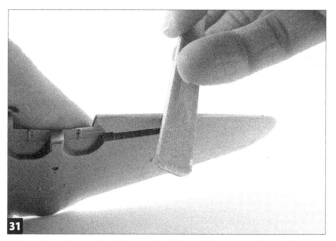

31 When cleaning up leading and trailing edge seams, keep the sanding stick moving so as not to create flat spots.

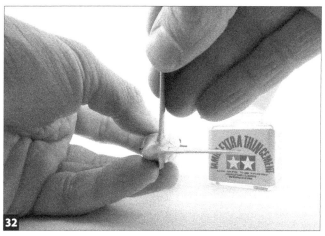

32 Check and recheck alignment before gluing on wings or stabilizers and don't be afraid to make adjustments as the glue sets.

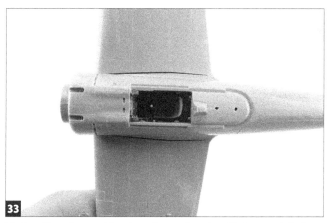

33 Mating the wing and fuselage is a major step. Unfortunately, I discovered large gaps at the wing roots on the Zero.

34 I held the wings up with tape as the glue dried, eliminating the gap and correcting the Zero's dihedral.

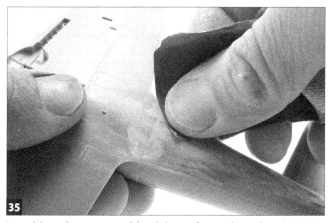

35 I used Squadron putty to blend the surfaces where the wing met the rear fuselage, a less-elegant solution.

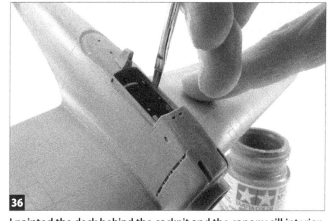

36 I painted the deck behind the cockpit and the canopy sill interior green before adding the canopy.

runs. Tamiya acrylics dry quickly, but it is still a good idea to wait several hours or overnight before painting over them.

The next day, I airbrushed Tamiya IJN gray green, starting with corners such as the wing roots, **43**. This ensures good coverage while minimizing the chances of too-heavy paint. Satisfied that the hard-to-

reach areas were painted, I set the brush to a slightly wider spray pattern and covered broad areas of the wings and fuselage, **44**. Remember, you don't want to produce complete coverage on the first pass. Build up the paint in several light coats.

I describe the perfect airbrushed acrylic coat as a little bit of brinksmanship

because there's a fine line between just the right amount and too much paint. Under the Zero's port wing, I inadvertently applied what looks like excess paint, and I anticipated paint runs and sanding, **45**. I let the model sit nose down to dry. Several hours later, I couldn't tell where I had gone awry, **46**. Don't forget to spray the

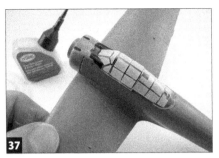

37 After masking with an Eduard precut mask set, I attached the three-part canopy with Testors Clear Parts Cement.

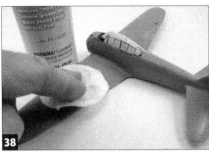

38 To prepare for painting, I wiped the airframe with Testors Surface Prep.

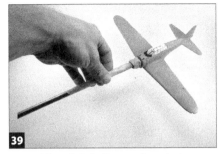

39 To avoid unsightly fingerprints during painting, I attached a brass-tube handle in the engine mount with poster putty.

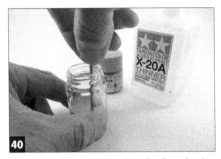

40 Stirred, not shaken, may make for a bad martini, but it is the best way to mix acrylic paint and thinner.

41 To ensure the canopy frame matches the interior, I first painted it cockpit green.

42 Using a scrap of sprue attached inside with poster putty, I airbrushed the cowl semigloss black.

43 Start spraying the body color in corners such as the wing root to aid coverage.

44 After adjusting the airbrush to a wider spray pattern, I finished painting the Zero.

45 I thought I was in trouble after getting a little too much paint under the wing.

parts that aren't attached to the model yet such as the landing gear doors, **47**.

Fixing blemishes. I've never put the first coat on a model without a bit of stray lint appearing, **48**. Don't be tempted to try and get it off the surface while the paint is wet. It always does more damage than good, and it's surprisingly easy to get rid of once the surface is dry. To do so, first try rubbing the surface with a soft cotton rag like an old T-shirt, **49**. It's unlikely to scratch or damage the paint, and you'll be amazed at how easy small particles are to remove. Failing that, lightly sand the spots with fine sandpaper, **50**. You want to remove the foreign object without adding deep scratches to the model. The paint revealed tiny gaps at the wing roots.

I used a toothpick to apply tiny amounts of super glue to fill the gap, **51**. Don't use accelerator to speed-dry here because it often attacks the paint.

Gloss coats and decals. Problems fixed, it was time for a second coat of paint, light sanding, and then a coat of Tamiya clear gloss thinned just like the other paint, **52**. With the addition of decals, the model is really starting to look like a real airplane. For information about decals, see page 32. Another coat of Tamiya gloss seals the decals and produces a good foundation for the artist's oil washes. Some modelers might see this as overkill, but I like to be sure turpentine or thinner doesn't get underneath the decals and affect adhesion.

Panel-line washes. For modelers, weathering refers to things done to a model to replicate the effects of weather as well as things like dry-brushing and washes that enhance a model's realism. Since the Zero I was building is a Pearl Harbor attacker, I figured it wouldn't have been especially worn or weary.

But I wanted to enhance its appearance with light weathering. First and foremost, I wanted to enhance the beautifully engraved panel lines with a wash of burnt umber artist's oil. I'm not a fan of overall washes, where you use a broad flat brush to apply wash over the whole model since most collects in engraved lines. I prefer a sort of hybrid between an overall wash and targeted pinwashes.

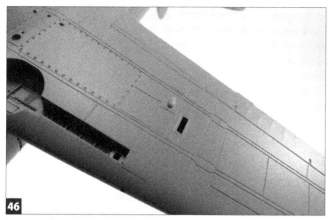

46

Whew! After several hours of drying, the pool of paint is nowhere to be seen.

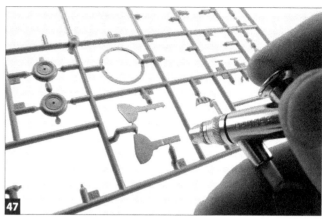

47

With the nozzle and pressure dialed down slightly, I painted the landing gear doors on the sprue.

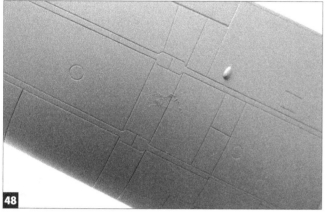

48

Dust and hair are every airbrusher's nemesis. This is the largest of several bits of flotsam that ended up stranded in the wet paint.

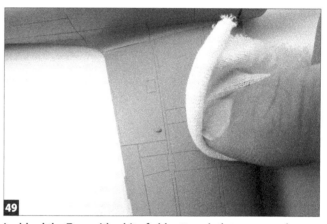

49

I rubbed the Zero with a bit of old cotton cloth to remove dust particles caught in the paint.

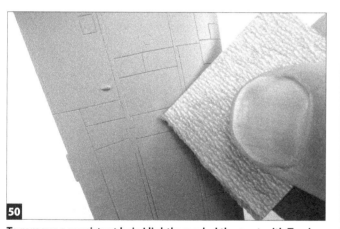

50

To remove a persistent hair, I lightly sanded the spot with Tamiya 1000-grit sandpaper.

51

The paint highlighted minor gaps at the wing root. I filled them with super glue on the head of a toothpick.

First, brush a thin coat of clear Turpenoid over the surface that the wash is about to be applied to, **53**. Then apply a 9:1 mix of Turpenoid and paint directly to the panel lines with a pointed brush, **54**. Capillary action should draw the thin paint an inch or so in each direction from where the brush touches. You don't have to be especially neat.

After a few minutes, dip a clean brush in clean thinner and blot it mostly dry on a paper towel. Drag the brush across the airframe in the direction of airflow (generally front to back) to remove most of the color outside the lines and to leave subtle streaks, **55**.

Washes can be built up in layers to create darker and lighter areas. I added more wash

to control surface boundaries to enhance the illusion of being separate parts. After several days drying time, apply clear flat, semigloss, or gloss, depending on your subject, to blend everything together, **56**. Be careful not to apply too much too fast as it can cloud.

Final details. After painting the landing gear bays and the inside of the gear doors

APPLYING DECALS

I've always enjoyed the moment I add decals to a model; to me, it's always seemed like the moment when the hunk of painted plastic takes a huge step toward reality. Markings give the model a scale reference as well as an immediate human connection. So decals are fun for me, but they can also be frustrating. Things can go wrong, and nothing ruins a masterpiece like bad decals. Following a few simple steps and tips can make decals easy.

Prepare the surface. Decals stick better on gloss paint, so if the base color is flat, spray the model with the clear gloss of your choice and let it dry.

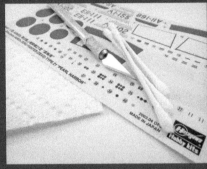
A fresh, sharp No. 11 blade, cotton swabs, and paper towels are the tools you need when working with decals.

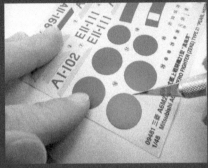
Decals are sealed with clear film that may extend past the edge of the marking and cause problems. Run a blade tip around the markings and cut through the film, not the paper. Separate the decal from the sheet with a knife or sharp scissors. Leave extra paper around the marking.

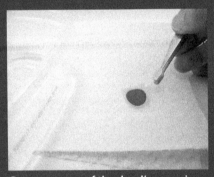
Grasp a corner of the decal's paper in flat-tip tweezers and dip the decal in warm water for a few seconds. Don't let it soak or the decal may float off the backing paper in the water. Set the wet decal on a piece of paper towel or another absorbent surface while the water activates the adhesive.

While the decal is on the paper towel, paint the model's surface with a setting solution. I prefer Microscale's two-part process: Micro Set and Micro Sol. These solutions are about the right strength for most decals. They cause decals to soften, settle into the recesses, and appear to be painted on the surface.

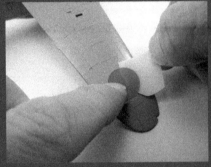
Use a toothpick to carefully move the excess carrier film from around the marking before moving the decal to the model. Hold the paper at the marking's location and gently slide the decal off the paper and into place.

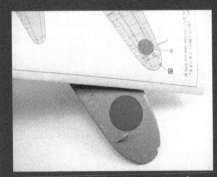
Double-check the location against the instructions and use reference points such as panel lines to refine the position. If the decal does not slide easily onto the surface, add a little water.

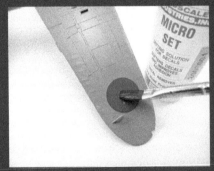
Once you're happy with the decal's location, brush more Micro Set onto the decal and let it sit for several minutes.

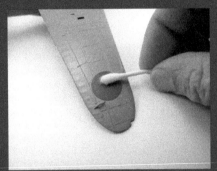
Gently press and blot the decal with a folded paper towel or roll a cotton swab across it to remove the setting solution and to push the decal into panel lines.

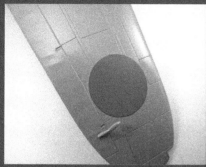

After the setting solution dried, it was obvious that the *hinomaru* on the Zero's wing wasn't settling into the panel lines as deeply as I wanted.

Micro Sol is stronger than Micro Set. I brushed it over the decal to soften it and help it settle into surface detail.

Don't be alarmed! As Micro Sol works, the decal will wrinkle. It looks bad but don't be tempted to touch it. Instead, leave it alone for several hours. The decal will level out as it dries.

Here's the same tail marking the next day. The wrinkles are gone and the panel lines are showing.

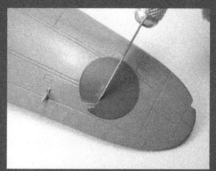

Sometimes decals have to go over prominent details such as the wing lights on the Zero. Carefully slit the decal over the obstacle and then brush on the setting solution.

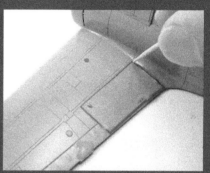

You can use a blunt toothpick to maneuver difficult decals into place but be careful not to tear them.

To help decals stick to compound curves, paint on a little thin white glue and press the marking into place.

When decals don't lay flat across the surface, air gets trapped underneath, causing a reflection known as silvering. This is common if you try to apply decals to flat instead of gloss paint.

You can correct silvering by poking tiny holes in the decal with a hobby knife and painting on setting solution so it settles through the holes and softens the decal into the surface.

Decal troubleshooting. There are a couple of things that can go wrong when applying decals. The one that will ruin your day is having a decal disintegrate when it hits the water. The cause is too little, too thin, or disintegrated clear coat. If one decal is toast, don't toss the whole sheet in the trash yet. You may be able to save the rest of the sheet by replacing the clear carrier. Microscale's Liquid Decal film can be applied by brush directly onto the sheet; it levels in the few minutes that it takes to dry. Testors makes a decal coat in a spray can. You can also airbrush a clear coat such as Model Master or Tamiya. After the decals are sealed, the downside is that the clear coat is continuous, so each marking will need to be trimmed closely. The other issue to watch for is setting solutions. Not all decals are created equally, and setting solutions that work well for one brand may not work on others. Some may be so strong that they will destroy the decal. Test setting solutions or solvents on an extra decal first. Also see if the weaker setting solutions will work alone without the stronger solvents.

52 Apply Tamiya clear gloss for a smooth surface for decals and weathering.

53 I wet the Zero's wing with clear thinner to promote paint flow and make the wash easier to control.

54 A fine pointed brush is the best way to apply a pinwash. I touched it to each screw head to ensure even coverage.

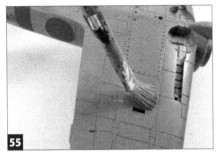

55 An almost dry brush of clean thinner drawn lightly over the surface removes excess wash.

56 Opening the nozzle for a wide pattern, I applied several light coats of Model Master Acryl flat clear for a more realistic sheen.

57 To replicate the distinct duck egg blue varnish applied to Japanese airframes, I mixed clear blue and clear green with clear gloss.

58 I touched up the canopy edges with a fine brush.

59 It's hard to find a better reflective surface for lights than Testors chrome silver enamel straight from the bottle.

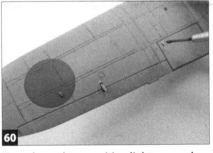

60 Zeros have three position lights on each wing. I painted those on the portside Tamiya clear red.

flat aluminum, I coated them with a 4:2:8 mix of Tamiya clear blue, clear green, and clear gloss, **57**. This is my interpretation of the tinted anticorrosion varnish used on Japanese aircraft early in World War II.

I removed the canopy masks and popped off the sliding section and then touched up the canopy edges and ends, **58**. Remember to paint interior edges the cockpit color.

I painted the inside of the wingtip light cutouts and the four lights on top of the wing Testors chrome silver enamel, **59**. The small clear wingtip globes needed to be trimmed and sanded to fit, but they look better if they don't stand out from the surface. I attached them with thin Testors Clear Parts Cement and then coated

the portside lights with Tamiya clear red and the starboard lights clear blue, **60**. I've found the best way to use Tamiya's clear colors is to pick up a small blob on the tip of a small brush—enough to cover the light but not get out of hand—and touch it to the light. Surface tension pulls the color over the lens.

I attached the rest of the small parts (antenna, landing-gear legs and doors, engine, and cowl guns) with small dabs of super glue. Keep the model well away from the glue supply while doing this and apply the smallest amount of adhesive needed to avoid spoiling the surface. I rarely bother trying to remove the paint from all the attachment points during this phase; if you use the right amount

of super glue, it will hold the parts, and there's little risk of harming the finish. If you get glue where you don't want it, don't wipe it off wet, or you'll smear it further and do more damage. Instead, wait a few minutes and lightly and carefully flatten the blob with fine sandpaper. I touched up any bare plastic with fine brushes and a light touch.

The propeller shaft was too big for the hole in the engine, **61**, so I bored the hole out with a pin vise.

The cowl tightly fit the fuselage, so I simply pushed it into place rather than gluing it. Then I installed the propeller with a little super glue.

Because this Zero flew December 7, 1941, I wanted it clean. But I wanted it to

61

The final stumbling block—a too-small hole in the engine for the prop shaft—was easily solved with a pin vise.

62

I ground a stick of dark brown pastel against coarse sandpaper to create a small pile of powder.

63

Using an old paint brush trimmed short, lightly brush pastels to produce exhaust streaks. Pastels adhere best to flat finishes.

Early-war Zeros, such as my model, were well maintained and kept clean. With no color camouflage to add, the A6M2 makes a good starter model.

look operational, not museum shiny, so I added a little exhaust streaking behind the pipes under the nose. To do so, grind little piles of dark brown and light gray chalk pastels on sandpaper, **62**. Apply the brown powder with a soft round brush

streaking back from the exhaust in the airflow, **63**. Work slowly and build up the effect. Blow excess pastel off rather than trying to rub it off.

The last touch is adding an antenna wire from the top of the mast to the top of the tail.

You can stretch sprue or use invisible thread. Stretching sprue is done by heating it with a candle flame and carefully pulling it and attaching it with super glue or white glue.

After completing the final details, you can sit back and admire your handiwork.

5

Getting a Jump-start on
AUTOMOBILES

Skills

- Car-building techniques
- Priming
- Applying gloss finishes
- Flocking
- Working with foil

W hile painting is always important for modelers, finish is everything. Gloss paint has challenges that flat finishes usually found on military subjects don't. Nothing ruins a beautifully built car like a bad paint job. I think disappointing finishes stop a lot of modelers from building cars. Truth is, like any other modeling skill, it can be mastered with practice.

I built a Tamiya 1/24 scale Morris Mini Cooper 1275S. I love the real car, and, for now, this is as close as I can get to owning one. Car models come in two types: curbside with no engine and fully detailed with an engine and an opening hood. Tamiya's Mini is the latter. It features plated parts for the bumpers, grille, and headlight bezels; soft rubber tires; and decals for instrument faces and British and Japanese license plates.

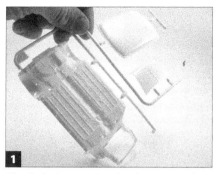

1

Check the instructions for the parts to be painted the body color. On the Mini, that includes the body shell, hood, under pan, and door panels. I missed the dashboard/firewall the first time around and had to paint it separately.

2

Make sure to prime the body inside and out since much of the interior is the body color. Also, on the Mini, there are two panels on each side that need to be gray, so with gray primer, you can kill two birds with one stone.

3

Even the nicest kits need a little attention. Primer exposed fine raised mold seams on the body.

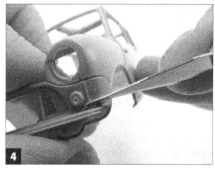

4

Lightly drag a No. 11 blade along the seam to remove the plastic ridge. Work carefully so you do not remove too much plastic.

5

Fine sandpaper smooths inconsistencies left by the knife.

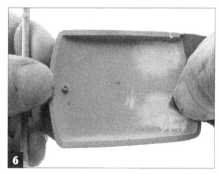

6

I removed ejector-pin marks under the roof with 400-, 600-, and 1000-grit sandpaper.

Surface preparation. The body is everything on a car, so I always start by painting it. Before even choosing the finish, I separated the parts that would be painted the body color, **1**. Next, I bathed the parts in a mild solution of dishwashing soap and lukewarm water to remove any mold-release agent or finger oil. You can pat the parts dry but let them stand for a few hours to be sure all the water is gone; even the smallest trace trapped in a crevice can cause painting problems. Finally, I wiped the body with Testors Plastic Prep.

Priming and cleanup. I primed the Mini with Mr. Surfacer 1000 straight from the spray can, **2**. It's a good primer for car bodies as it produces a velvety smooth finish that's thick enough to fill fine abrasions in the surface.

Although Tamiya's parts are very clean, the initial primer coat revealed fine mold seams on each corner, **3**. I removed them by scraping along the ridge with a No. 11 blade, **4**. Light sanding finished the job and blended the area, **5**. I also rubbed the rest of the body with 1000-grit sand-

paper to knock off any dust or hair and to smooth the primer. Don't worry about exposing the plastic at this stage because there's another layer of primer to come. The primer also showed how obvious the ejector-pin marks under the roof were, so I took time to sand that area smooth, **6**. Finally, I sprayed the body with a light coat of Mr. Surfacer to cover the bare plastic and lightly sanded the surface.

Painting gloss. I started by spray-painting the roof with Tamiya pure white while holding it on a brass-rod handle attached with a big blob of poster putty.

Creating gloss finishes is a matter of careful paint application. Hold the nozzle 6"–8" above the surface to be sprayed and start and finish each pass off the model. Start with just enough quick passes to deposit a mist of paint over the surface, **7**. After 10–15 minutes, apply a

7

The first pass is about getting a little paint on all surfaces, not about complete coverage. Mist the paint on and then let the part sit for 10–15 minutes.

8

Good gloss paint is reflective. Notice the compact florescent bulb reflected in the white paint.

9

Having chosen Tamiya light blue for the Mini, I taped a drinking straw to the spray can's nozzle. Make sure there are no leaks around the straw's base to prevent messy leaks.

10

Keep the hole in the plastic wrap as small as possible to minimize paint splattering out of the container during decanting.

11

Although I'm not wearing gloves in the photo, I recommend them during decanting to protect your hands from paint splatters.

12

Propellant boiling out of the decanted paint shows up as bubbles in the paint.

more complete coat, this time looking for complete coverage. Check for dust or other debris in the paint between coats. If any shows up, remove it by rubbing the surfaces with a soft cloth immediately before the next coat.

After waiting another 10–15 minutes, apply a wet coat. Keep the can moving over the surface to prevent excessive paint buildup and unsightly runs,

but move slow enough to put the right amount of paint on the surface. It should look wet and smooth on the surface after each pass. You can check the finish by looking at a light bulb's reflection in the paint; it should be a perfect reflection if the paint has leveled out nicely, **8**. Place the part under a cover or hang it with the painted side down to prevent dust from settling in the fresh paint as it dries.

Decanting spray paint. Spray cans produce very high volumes of paint that can be very hard to control, especially when trying to get paint inside tight spots. Airbrushes solve this problem, but they don't always produce the right amount of paint for smooth finishes. The solution is to combine the two application methods to best advantage, using the airbrush to paint corners and

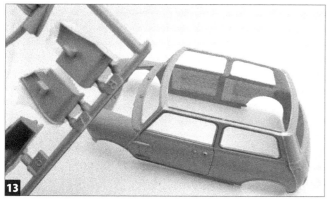

13 I trimmed strips of Tamiya tape to mask the inside of the body before painting it.

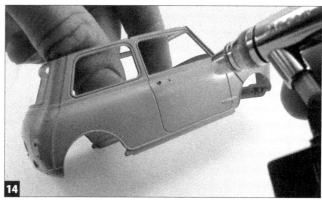

14 The Mini's body is relatively uncomplicated, but it still has areas that can benefit from prepainting with an airbrush.

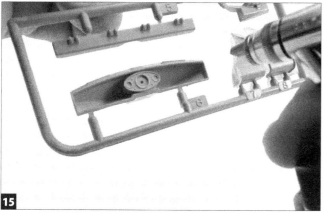

15 Don't forget small parts still on the tree, such as the dash and door panels, that need to be painted with the airbrush.

16 Hold the body with a paint stand—even a bent wire coat hanger will work—so you can move the model without touching it. Remember to start and finish painting off the model.

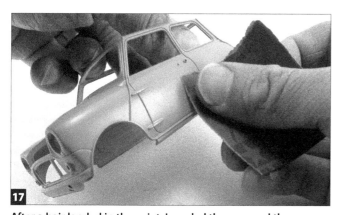

17 After a hair landed in the paint, I sanded the area and then applied a light coat of paint.

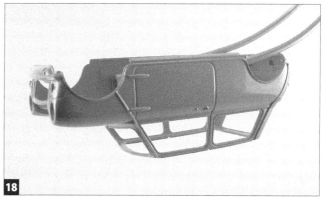

18 Dust is a painter's nemesis. To keep it blemish free, I suspended the Mini upside down under a cover while the finish dried.

crevices and using the spray can for major coverage. To be sure the paint matches, it's necessary to decant the spray can, so you can spray it through an airbrush.

First, tape a 2"–3" piece of a plastic drinking straw securely over the nozzle on the spray can, **9**. You'll need a container to catch the paint. I used an old pill container with plastic wrap stretched taut across the mouth and held in place with a rubber band. A small hole in the plastic wrap finishes the job, **10**.

Shake the paint can vigorously to be sure the paint deposited in the container is the correct consistency. Then insert the straw in the container and depress the spray can's nozzle. Paint will quickly run out of the end of the straw and begin filling the container, **11**.

Resist the temptation to airbrush the decanted paint immediately. It will be filled with suspended propellant that can produce bubbles in the paint on the model, **12**. Instead, loosely cap the container and let it stand for at least 12 hours. Don't cap it tight, or you may get an explosion of paint when you open the container because of built-up pressure.

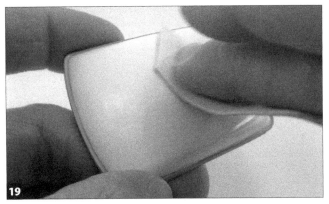

19 Buff the paint with progressively finer sanding pads. Work in a circular pattern, don't press too hard, and stay clear of ridges or panel edges to avoid exposing primer or plastic.

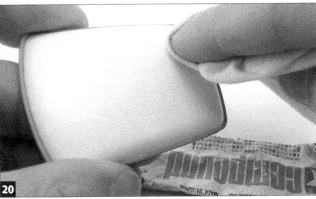

20 Apply polish with a soft cotton cloth, rub in small circles until a haze appears, and then buff the paint with a clean cloth.

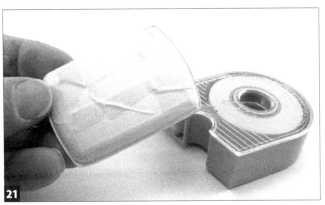

21 When masking, burnish the tape edge tight against the paint edges to prevent paint bleeding. Also check seams between tape strips to eliminate gaps where paint might slip through.

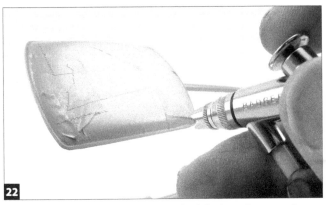

22 The Mini's roof gutter is narrow and might have been easily overwhelmed by paint straight from a spray can. I used an airbrush set to a narrow paint pattern.

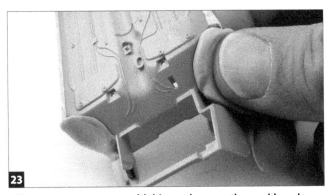

23 Silly Putty may seem an odd thing to keep on the workbench, but it's perfect for masking irregular shapes such as wheel wells.

24 To remove stubborn Silly Putty, push a blob of the stuff into it, and roll or pull it off.

Spraying the body. Now's the time to mask any areas of the body that are to remain gray. On the Mini, that included the padded panels inside the doors and those next to the rear seat, **13**.

Pour some of the decanted paint into the airbrush bottle and spray hard to reach areas: inside wheel wells, around doors and windows, along rocker panels, by trim and accent lines and ridges, and in license plate and grille recesses, **14**. Make

sure you lay down a solid layer of paint now, so you don't have to cover with the spray can. Paint the small parts with the airbrush as well, **15**.

Grab the spray can and spray the body before the prepainted areas have a chance to dry, **16**. Use the three-step method as done in painting the roof—mist, cover coat, and wet coat—to get a smooth finish. If necessary, sand any rough spots between coats, **17**. Then, hang the body

upside down under a cover to keep dust out of the paint while it dries, **18**.

On a modern car, I will usually apply clear gloss over the paint. On the Mini, the paint looked right for a 1960s car, so I skipped that stage.

Ideally, if you have gotten the paint right, it should level out and appear glass smooth and reflective. The closer it is at this stage, the less sanding, rubbing, and polishing you'll need to do. If the surface isn't

25 Check the parts on the sprues before painting and remove any mold seams with a hobby knife and sandpaper.

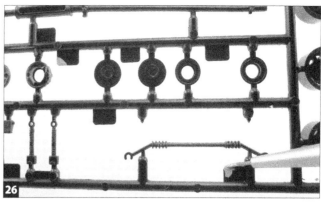

26 To find parts for airbrushing, mark them on the sprue with a color you can easily see. Permanent markers can also be used.

27 Tamiya NATO black, actually a very dark gray, is a great color for rubber such as the steering and suspension boots.

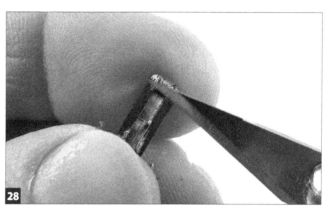

28 I scraped the chrome plating from the gluing surface on the cylinder head, so solvent-based glue could be used to attach it.

29 Tamiya molds tiny bumps where the plugs are located on the block. I twisted the tip of a No. 11 blade at the head of each bump to start the hole and prevent the bit from slipping.

30 I dipped one end of the ignition wires into a puddle of thick super glue. The tacky gel holds the wires in the holes as it sets, so you don't have to babysit them as the glue dries.

smooth enough, you can buff the paint with special pads from LMG or MicroMesh or even with a nail buffer, **19**. I used Tamiya polishing compound, **20**, and Mike's Scale Speed Shop Slick 'N' Smooth Polish to get a nice deep shine.

Masking for details. Parts of the Mini's roof and chassis needed to be painted other colors which means masking. For the roof's rain gutter, which was

going to be light blue, I stretched and trimmed Tamiya masking tape around the edge before covering the rest, **21**. Use a sharp No. 11 blade to cut the tape at the perimeter, so you don't have to press hard and damage the paint. I airbrushed the edge with decanted paint, **22**.

The chassis was awkward because most of the areas to be masked are far from straight. I masked the rocker panels with strips of tape but used Silly Putty for

the wheel wells, **23**. Silly Putty is great for this. It sticks but not enough to damage paint, and it can be pushed into tight spaces and odd shapes. It's easy to remove but it can stick to itself better than the model, **24**. I painted the chassis Tamiya semigloss black acrylic.

Painting details. Tamiya provides a nice replica of the Mini's tiny power plant, drive train, and suspension. I airbrushed

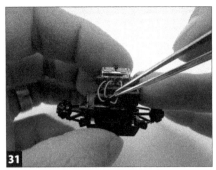

31

Using long, pointed tweezers makes handling and connecting the wires to the distributor easy.

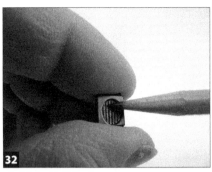

32

The humble pencil is a great way to represent metal.

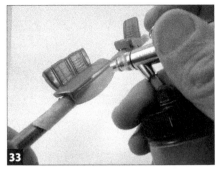

33

The light blue-black mix I used for the seats produced a semigloss sheen that looks a lot like vinyl.

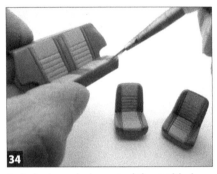

34

A dark pinwash deepened the molded cushion detail, which made the seats look better when seen through the windows and gave them a used appearance.

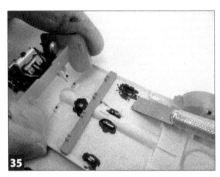

35

Hold the knife so the bevel is flat against the surface and the handle is up. Work the chisel blade through the base, rocking back and forth if necessary. (Never carve toward your hand as I'm doing here.)

36

I brushed on a thin layer of white glue a section at a time.

most of the parts on the sprue before construction, but many needed mold seams removed with a hobby knife and sandpaper, **25**. To ensure I painted them the right colors without missing any, I placed a dab of easy-to-see light green paint on the part number next to the parts to be painted semigloss black, **26**. Make sure you turn the tree around so you get paint on every surface. I brush-painted details such as the rubber boots on the steering rack, **27**.

I painted the engine Tamiya NATO green and added the chrome-plated head, **28**. Be sure to scrape paint and plating from any mating surfaces so solvent-based glues and super glues work.

Wiring the engine. Tamiya's engine is pretty complete, but it lacks wiring, including the prominent ignition lines that are front and center. To add these, I first drilled holes in the four spark plug locations on the engine block and on the distributor with a No. 80 bit in a pin vise, **29**.

I cut four pieces of Detail Master 1/24 scale ignition wire longer than they need-

ed to be and glued each into the spark plug holes with super glue gel, **30**. After several minutes—the glue needs to be cured before the next stage—I used tweezers to bend each wire down to meet the distributor, **31**. I followed by adding a wire from the coil to the distributor after the engine was mounted in the compartment.

I toned down the chrome head with a brushed coat of Model Master Acryl clear flat and applied a light raw umber artist's oil wash to weather the engine. I wanted my Mini to represent an everyday commuter, rather than a show car. To highlight the molded radiator detail and give it a metallic sheen, I rubbed the painted part with a No. 2 pencil, **32**.

Upholstery. After removing prominent mold seams from the seats, I primed them with Mr. Surfacer 1000, a good match for the center panels of the Mini's two-tone fabric. I masked the gray areas with Tamiya tape. The other parts of the seats are a close match to the body color. I mixed a little Tamiya black spray lacquer with some of the decanted light blue for

a slightly darker shade, **33**. A dark brown artist's oil wash emphasized the molded detail, **34**. The floor has several locators for seats used in another version of the kit. I carved them away with a chisel blade, **35**.

Several companies sell flocking to reproduce the carpet found in most cars, but I used embossing powder instead. Embossing powder is made up of tiny pellets that look like low pile carpet, whereas flocking is made up of long fibers that makes for great show car carpet. Either way the application is the same. I painted white glue on the area to be carpeted, **36**. Then I poured a little more of the embossing powder than I needed into the wet glue, flipping and turning the floor so the powder was distributed to every section, **37**. The dry embossing powder takes paint very well, **38**. Before adding the dashboard to the interior, I applied the instrument face decals and sealed them with glass made by dripping in 5-minute epoxy, **39**.

Applying foil. Nothing looks quite like metal, except metal. I used Testors chrome silver enamel for some of the Mini's small-

37 Move the embossing powder around the floor to achieve an even distribution. Then flip it over and tap it to get rid of the excess.

38 I painted the carpet Tamiya dark sea gray with a large, flat brush. Let the paint soak into the surface for good coverage.

39 It's easy to replicate glass with 5-minute epoxy because it dries crystal clear. Drip a blob into the bezel and let it settle as it dries.

40 To apply self-adhesive foil, use a fresh No. 11 blade and a cotton swab. The blade must be sharp to avoid tearing the delicate foil.

er metal items like door handles. For larger items, like the metal trim around the windows, I turned to self-adhesive foil, **40**. Specifically I used Bare-Metal Foil, which is offered in several shades. I used flat aluminum rather than chrome because I felt the slightly duller shade better replicated the trim on the full-size car.

Start by cutting out a piece of foil slightly larger than the area to be covered and remove it from the backing paper with the tip of the knife, **41**. Place the foil on the model so it overlaps the area on all sides. Then, start pressing the foil into and around the surface detail, **42**. To open the window, cut through the foil leaving a fraction of an inch, a little more than the thickness of plastic, around the edge, **43**. Fold the foil around the frame with a finger and burnish it with a cotton swab to be sure it conforms to the surface and sticks well, **44**.

Next, run the tip of a round toothpick around the frame to push the foil into the outline, **45**, and use a No. 11 blade to trim the excess, **46**. It should be a simple

matter to grasp a corner of the foil and peel it away from the model, **47**. I used a Sharpie permanent marker to draw on the rubber seals for the windshield and rear window, **48**.

Windows and final assembly. After I removed the windows from the sprue with a razor saw, I glued them into the body shell with Testors Clear Parts Cement and Window Maker thinned with water, **49**. The Mini's long side windows were slightly warped, so I held them in place with short masking tape strips until the glue dried, **50**.

Many rubber or vinyl tires have a mold seam in the center of the tread, **51**. This can usually be removed with a sharp knife or razor blade or by sanding as I did on the Mini. Tamiya's rubber looks about right, but some kit tires are very shiny and hitting them with sandpaper will produce a realistic sheen.

I painted the back of turn signal and taillights, molded in clear plastic, with Model Master chrome silver and painted

the lenses Tamiya clear orange and clear red. Apply these paints in relatively heavy single coats to get good color density and to minimize brush strokes. The headlights, taillights, and indicators were attached to the body with Testors Clear Parts Cement.

The only fit problem I had with the Mini came when I slipped the body over the chassis and interior. The internal panels for the doors don't have any locator pins, and they ended up slightly too far forward, which prevented a clean fit. I had attached the panel with super glue and was able to pop them off and move them back a fraction of an inch. Unfortunately, during construction super glue fumes clouded the driver's side window, **52**. Resisting the temptation to throw the model down the stairs, I grabbed a cotton swab dipped in isopropyl alcohol and rubbed the window, eliminating most of the haze.

I attached the few remaining parts with tiny spots of super glue gel. My Mini was finished—almost.

CLEAR PART CLARITY

Clear styrene is different from other plastic used in model kits, and it should be handled carefully to avoid scratching or marring and ruining you masterpiece. As if it's not bad enough that you can't easily hide problems on clear plastic, it tends to be brittle and more easily scratched than opaque plastic.

Clear plastic's brittleness means it's easily distorted or cracked around the sprue attachment point during part removal. You can use sprue cutters but cut well away from the part to avoid damage. I prefer to use a saw to gently sever the connection. Work slowly and deliberately, watching exactly where the blade travels to prevent scratches. And keep a hand under the part, so when the part is free, it doesn't fall under your feet or the wheels of your chair. Ugly!

To remove the nub at the attachment point, first shave it off with a brand new hobby knife blade. Again, caution is the watchword. Keep an eye on where the tip of the blade is at all times and keep it on the stub. One slip could really mess up the part. Finally, use the edge of a fine-grit sanding stick to eliminate any trace of the attachment point. I may seem like I'm repeating myself, but work carefully to ensure that the sanding stick doesn't stray.

Correcting scratches and scuffs. Canopies and windshields are the focal points of aircraft and car models, and nothing takes away from a realistic finish like unclear clear parts. So what do you do if one of the clear parts in your kit gets damaged? Well, you could buy another kit, but the cheaper alternative is rubbing out the problem. This technique can also be used to remove mold seams found on some complex-shaped parts such as blown canopies.

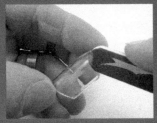   

| Start with the coarsest section and sand in small circles with a three-grit polishing stick to remove the blemish. | The sanded area will have a hazy appearance, which will smooth out by using the next finest grit. | Then, use the buffing surface to return the part's original luster. | A final polish using Novus No. 2 Fine Scratch Remover on a clean, soft cloth makes the part look better than new. |

Clear parts and Pledge Future. Sold for years as a no-mop floor finish, Pledge Future is a clear acrylic that dries rock hard and glossy. Future gives clear parts a brilliant shine, it protects the plastic from super glue fumes and fogging, and it also seems to make masks easier to remove. The easiest way to apply it is by dipping the parts one by one in the liquid.

| Remove each clear part from the tree, but leave a short piece of sprue attached to serve as a handle. | Fill a container with Future. To avoid bubbles forming, unscrew the top and slowly pour the polish in rather than using the bottle's squirt nozzle. | Holding the sprue with tweezers, gently submerge the part in the Future and then pull it out slowly to allow excess liquid to flow off. |

| Drag a corner of the part across a paper towel to remove some of the Future. Avoid touching large, flat surfaces. | You can sop up excess liquid in corners with a soft paintbrush. Then hang the part under a cover to stop dust from settling. |

Masking canopies. Remember brush-painting canopies as a kid? Mine were always uneven and tended to ruin my otherwise mediocre models. That's why precise masking is so important.

I use three methods depending on the size and complexity of the canopy being masked: tape, self-adhesive foil, and precut masks.

I prefer Tamiya's thin yellow tape because it's easy to cut, and you can see through to the surface, making trimming easy. Apply a piece of tape to a sheet of glass and cut a strip ⅓₂" wide.

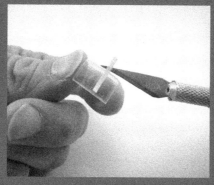

Transfer a short piece of this strip to the canopy with the tip of a No. 11 blade, aligning the edge with the engraved frame.

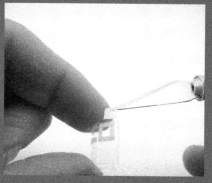

Trim the piece to length by running the point of the knife along the engraved line. Once the tape outline is in place, fill the void with tape.

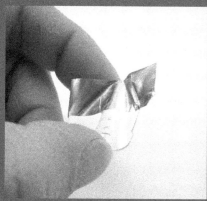

Bare-Metal Foil is self-adhesive, conforms easily to complex shapes, and is thin so framing detail shows up well underneath it. Cut a section slightly bigger than the area you plan to mask and apply it to the canopy.

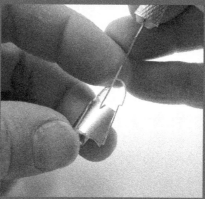

Burnish it over details, so raised and engraved lines are obvious and then trim along those lines with a new blade. Peel away the foil on the areas to be painted.

Available from manufacturers such as Eduard and True Details, and similar to Tamiya masking tape, precut masks fit perfectly and are easy to use. Carefully peel up the section you need with the point of a No. 11 blade.

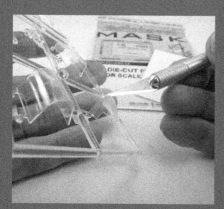

Align the mask with the engraved frame and press down with a cotton swab or burnishing tool for a tight seal.

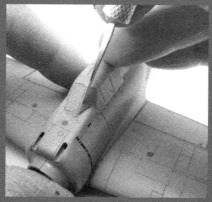

Whatever you use to mask, run the edge of a blade along the mask outline before removing it to break the paint seal.

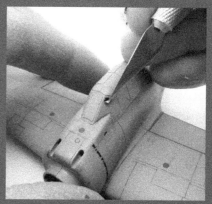

Then, slowly peel the mask off the canopy, pulling down and away from the surface.

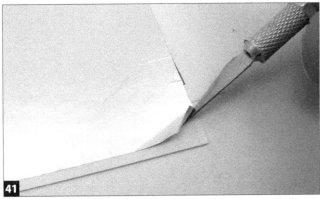

41

Gently slip the tip of the blade between the foil and paper at a corner. Peel the foil away, leaving the corner stuck to the knife, and transfer it to the model.

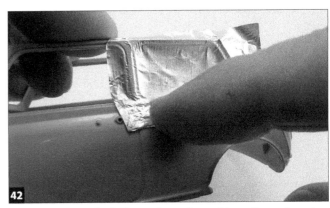

42

After smoothing the foil over the surface with my finger, I used a fingernail to push it into the groove around the window frame. Work slowly and gently.

43

Once most of the foil was removed from the window, I cut through the remainder at the corners.

44

I prefer cotton swabs to burnishing tools because the cushioning protects the foil. To avoid stray cotton fibers, use a fresh swab if the one you are using begins to fray.

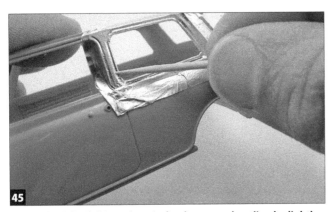

45

I burnished the foil into the window's recessed outline by lightly running the tip of a round toothpick around the frame. Drag, don't push!

46

Press just hard enough to slice through the thin foil so as not to cut into the paint. A sharp blade is essential as a dull blade will tear rather than cut.

The personal touch. One of the great things about building cars is personalizing the model. I know I'll never own a Spitfire or a T-72, but I drive a car every day. And there are things in every vehicle I've owned that mark it as mine. All I needed for adding those things to the model were a computer with simple photo editing software, a color printer, and some white decal paper.

The kit comes with right-hand drive, so I decided to make the Mini's home my hometown, Brisbane, Australia. First, I created a couple of personalized license plates in 1/24 scale and found a photo of a Queensland registration sticker for the windshield. I also added several bumper stickers to the back window.

I applied a decal of the Brisbane street directory cover to .030" styrene and placed it between the windshield and dash. There's a copy of *FineScale Modeler* on the passenger seat, as well as a selection of compact disks (Hoodoo Gurus, anyone?). Now, my Mini is ready for a road trip.

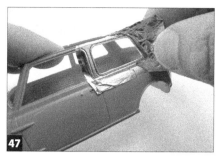

47 Peel excess foil slowly back against itself and watch for any unsevered connections that may tear the foil on the window.

48 It takes a steady hand but drawing windshield gaskets with a marker is easier and neater than trying to do it with masking tape and airbrushing or brush-painting. The semigloss, not-quite-black sheen looks like rubber.

49 I slipped the windows into place and painted thin clear part cement around the part letting capillary action pull the adhesive into the gap. Applying the glue after the part is in position minimizes the chance of glue marring the window.

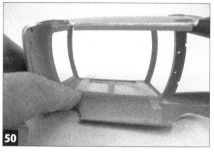

50 I lightly pressed tape into position on either end of the side windows to counter the warp as the glue set.

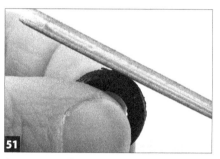

51 A coarse sanding stick makes quick work of the little ridge of flash along the mold seam in the middle of the tread on the Mini's tires.

52 Here's why detectives use super glue to reveal fingerprints—the fumes are attracted to skin oils. It's also why super glue is not a recommended adhesive for clear parts.

I personalized my Mini with Queensland, Australia, plates and other details. The model takes up little shelf space when displayed.

6

Launching Your First SHIP

Skills

- Working with small parts
- Masking
- Rigging
- Maritime weathering

hips are big. A *Nimitz*-class carrier is more than 1,000 feet long, and even a Royal Navy *Tribal-*class destroyer measures 377 feet. Big subjects mean small scales when it comes to models, and ship kits routinely range from 1/96 to 1/1200 scale. The two most common today are 1/700 and 1/350. So what does this mean for modelers? Two things: ships can still be relatively big models—a *Nimitz* carrier at 1/350 scale is more than 3 feet long— and there are going to be lots of small parts.

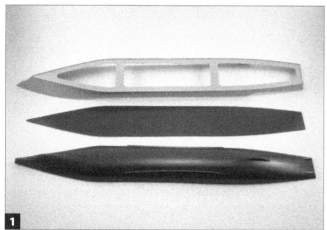

1 Trumpeter's USS *Cole* includes the option of building the model with a full hull or waterline with two pieces of maroon plastic. Some ship kits come as one or the other.

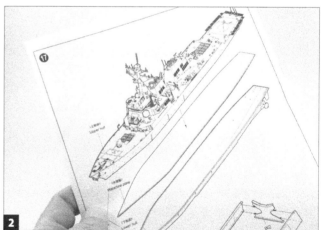

2 Major construction and small parts don't mix. Instead of building the hull in the last step, do it first.

Construction sequence. Ship modeling, like any genre, involve specific skills, but basic modeling skills can produce a good-looking model. There are no hard and fast rules on how to build a ship; each vessel type is different, so the way you build it will change a little. The best rule of thumb is to work bottom to top and from the inside out. In other words, build the hull first followed by the deck. Then work up through the superstructure from the inside out, painting each area as you go because there's a good chance you won't be able to reach a lot of areas once all the parts are in place.

Start by looking at the instructions. I built Trumpeter's 1/350 scale USS *Cole*, and right away, I noticed an issue in the sequence. The kit has the option of being built with either a full hull or as a waterline model, **1**. (Waterline replaces the lower hull, the part usually underwater when the vessel is at sea, with a flat plate

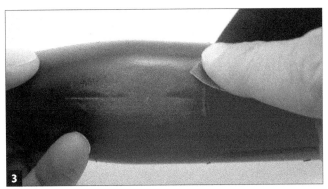

3

The hull parts are cast from multipart molds, which means you will have to clean up mold seams. The ridges aren't particularly large, but at 1/350 scale, they definitely needed to be removed.

4

A finger is a good tool for checking the joint; if there's a step between the parts, it'll be obvious, and you can move the parts in relation to each other.

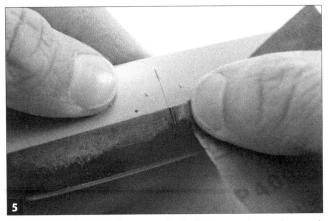

5

Fill and sand the seam between the hulls. Be sure to sand around the raised ribs that cross the waterline.

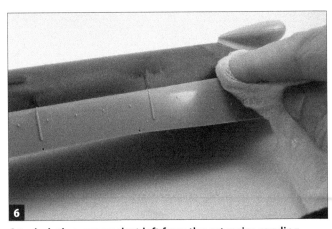

6

A tack cloth removes dust left from the extensive sanding needed to repair gaps and steps at the hull seam.

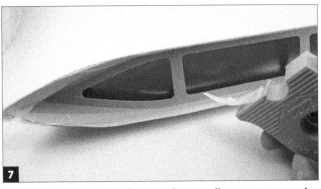

7

When masking gluing surfaces, make sure all areas are covered but check that the tape doesn't overlap the area to be painted.

8

I sprayed the hull neutral gray, making sure the color extended below the waterline.

so it appears to be floating on a shelf.) I planned to build a full hull version, but the hull parts are not joined until the final step in the instructions, **2**. Unless the fit is perfect, and dry-fitting proved it wasn't, that meant that there would be a lot of manhandling to fill, sand, mask, and paint with all the delicate fiddly bits attached. So the last step became the first.

The hull. I cleaned up mold seams at the bow and stern, along the keel, and around

the lower hull strakes, **3**. For a strong join and to allow time to adjust the fit, I used Testors liquid cement and checked the fit as I went, **4**. Despite my best efforts, the hull seam needed cleanup including filling, sanding, and scraping, **5**. After adding the propeller shafts, rudders, and bow sonar housing, I cleaned up those joints and ran a tack cloth over the hull to remove sanding residue, **6**. Before painting, I masked the deck gluing surfaces inside the edge, **7**.

Hull painting. Modern U.S. Navy ships like the *Cole* are painted haze gray, a color that can be found in several manufacturers' catalogs, but neutral gray is also a match. I airbrushed the hull with Model Master neutral gray, concentrating on the hull sides but making sure the gray overlapped the waterline, **8**. After the gray had several days to dry, I masked the upper hull by running a tape edge at the waterline, **9**. Then I airbrushed Polly Scale special oxide red, a good match for the

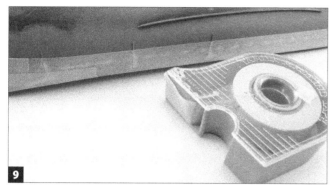

9 I used Tamiya 14mm tape to mask along the waterline at what will be the upper edge of the boot stripe. Take time to get the tape straight as any unevenness will ruin the effect.

10 Spray a light coat along the tape's edge to help seal the mask and then fill in the rest. Avoid spraying too much at the mask or you risk paint bleeding under the tape or forming a ridge.

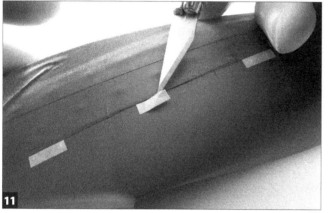

11 I used the tip of a hobby knife to place ³⁄₃₂" strips of tape on the waterline, butting them against the tape masking the upper hull.

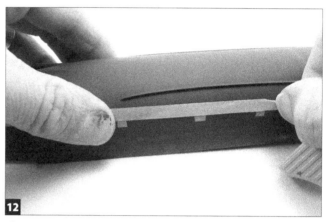

12 Placing tape along the opposite edge of the spacing strips sets a consistent width for the boot stripe along the hull.

13 Next, remove the tape strips from the gap and spray black for the boot topping.

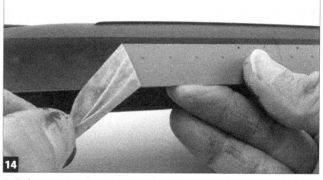

14 Pull the tape back against itself at about a 45 degrees angle from the masked edge to minimize chipping or damaging the paint.

anti-fouling paint on Navy ships, **10**. I left the tape on the model for the next stage.

The boot stripe. Most vessels have a black stripe, known as either a boot top or boot stripe, along the waterline. Getting the width correct and keeping it consistent along the hull can be a challenge. Just finding correct dimensions can be tough. After looking at photos, I decided around ³⁄₃₂" was about right. I cut strips of tape that width and placed them

along the mask for the gray at regular intervals, **11**. Then I ran tape along the other edge of the strips, **12**. I removed the spacing strips from the gap, **13**, and sprayed Tamiya NATO black along the line. I removed the tape soon after painting to minimize paint buildup along the masked lines, **14**.

Building the superstructure. Trumpeter has you assemble both *Cole's* superstructures from separate walls and roofs. I held

each together and applied liquid cement from the inside, **15**. Cleanup was easy; I ran sandpaper or the edge of a blade along the outside edge of the seam to remove excess plastic squeezed out of the join, **16**. Be careful not to round corners that should be sharp by working in the direction of the walls. I filled gaps with super glue flowed along the edge with a toothpick. **17**. The bridge level of the ship is made up from clear parts. After installing them, I masked the level with thin

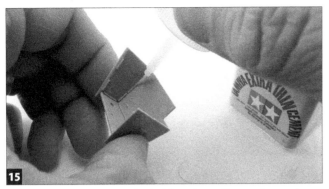

15 I built the superstructures by holding the walls together and flowing liquid cement from the inside.

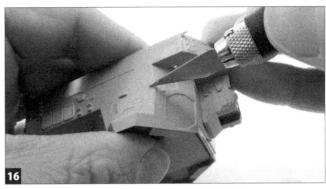

16 At the seams, any gaps or ridges will look out of place, and the delicate parts will be hard to clean up after painting.

17 Thin super glue is a perfect filler for ships. Apply it with a toothpick and let it flow along the gap and dry.

18 After building the bridge level, mask the windows with tape. Brush-painting at the end of the project will frame the panes.

19 Pay attention to the instructions. Small components like turrets are better assembled before painting.

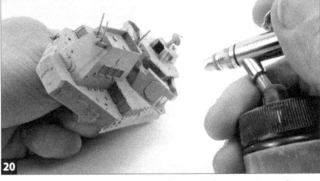

20 The superstructures are complex shapes. Take your time when painting to ensure full coverage, even in the deepest recesses.

strips of tape, **18**. I'll paint the thin frames between each window by hand at the end of the build. I built many of the small components—turret, CIWS (close-in weapon system) units, torpedo tubes, funnels—called for in the instructions, **19**.

Painting and details. I airbrushed the assembled structures neutral gray, **20**. I applied the same color to the parts still on the sprue, **21**, as well as the smaller components, which I secured to a tongue depressor with poster putty, **22**.

I airbrushed the two deck parts dark gull gray on the sprue, **23**, and then brush-painted the deck sections on the superstructure, **24**. Before attaching the main decks, I scraped paint from the attachment points for the superstructures, **25**. The decks were snug, and I attached them with liquid cement and left them to dry overnight. I taped the photoetched-metal frets to cardboard to paint them, **26**.

In the meantime, I added the small details to the superstructures, which are much easier to handle now before being attached to the 20"-long hull. The easiest way to add these little bits is to dip the ends in a puddle of thick super glue and then insert them in the locator holes, **27**.

For small parts like the life rafts, I picked them up with the tip of a No. 11 blade and positioned them on the racks, **28**.

Once all the parts were in position, I touched up sprue attachment points and areas of thin paint by brush-painting neutral gray, **29**. While I had the brush out, I painted small details like the white radar domes and CIWS tops. I lightened neutral gray with a few drops of white to paint the radar sensor panels around the bridge tower and used dark sea gray for the ship's numerous vent panels.

I added the superstructures to the deck with liquid cement. The front tower

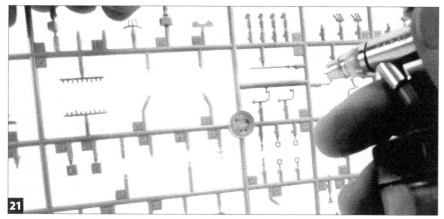

21 Very small parts are best painted on the sprue. Move the tree around to ensure coverage.

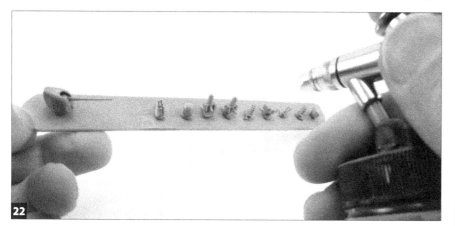

22 Tongue depressors or craft sticks make inexpensive handles when airbrushing small parts. Poster putty or double-sided tape secures the parts to the wood.

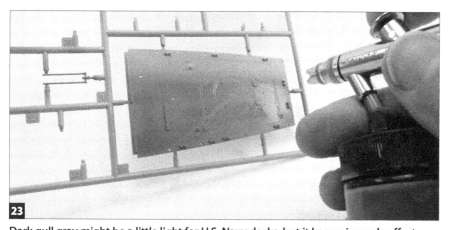

23 Dark gull gray might be a little light for U.S. Navy decks, but it has a nice scale effect.

USS *COLE*

One of 62 Arleigh Burke-class guided-missile destroyers, the USS Cole was launched in February 1995 and commissioned in June 1996. The ship is armed with a 5" gun in a turret and scores of missiles in two vertical launch emplacements fore and aft. It is equipped with an Aegis combat system that is capable of tracking more than 100 targets, and it carries two Phalanx close-in weapons system units to protect the ship from enemy missiles.

The USS *Cole* (DDG 67, *Arleigh Burke*-class guided missile destroyer) is at sea one month before being attacked by a terrorist-suicide mission during the early morning hours of October 12, 2000. *U. S. Navy photo*

On October 12, 2000, suicide bombers attacked the USS Cole in Aden, Yemen, with a boat packed with explosives. The blast ripped opened a 40' hole in the port hull, killing 17 sailors and injuring 39. After returning to the United States, the Cole underwent a 14-month repair. The ship returned to service in 2002, and it deployed overseas in November 2003 and in 2005, returning to the Middle East in 2006. The ship is named in honor of U.S. Marine machine gunner Sgt. Darrell S. Cole who was killed in action on Iwo Jima in February 1945.

needs to fit flush with the hull sides. It fit if I pressed down hard as I installed it, and I found that cutting the port side away from the rear wall slightly improved the fit there, **30**. I finished basic construction with the installation of all the small parts on the deck.

Installing photoetched railings. One of the best uses for photoetched metal is as railings on ship models. Plastic just can't

be molded thin enough to make a realistic railing. Adding photoetched-metal railings can appear daunting. Yes, it's challenging, and best not rushed, but all it takes is basic modeling skills and a couple of tools. (I used the set from the Trumpeter kit as well as a few photoetched-metal details from a Dragon 1/350 scale *Arleigh Burke*-class destroyer.) It's a good idea to work from the inside out, so you don't have to reach across already installed parts. This

minimizes the chances of damaging the work you've already done.

Some kits or aftermarket detail sets do a good job of informing the builder of the measurements for installing railings. Alas, Trumpeter didn't give any clues for the *Cole*. (In fact, there are no instructions

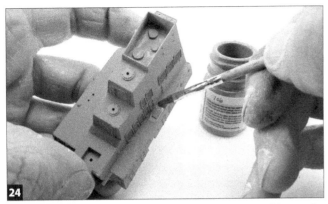

24

For small deck areas, brush-painting is easier than masking and airbrushing. I used a small chisel brush to paint around details.

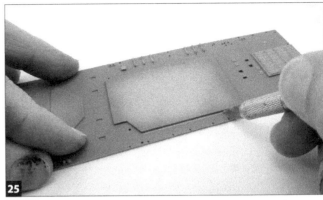

25

I used a small curved blade to scrape paint from the attachment points for the major structures on the deck.

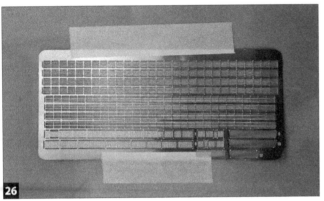

26

I painted the photoetched-metal parts before attaching them. The paint will chip off corners during assembly but can be touched up.

27

Thick super glue takes longer to set, but the higher viscosity holds the parts in position while it dries.

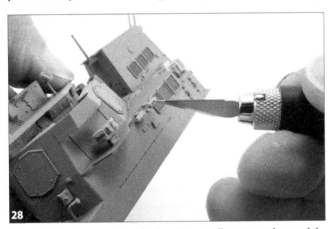

28

A new blade is a great tool for locating small parts on the model. Just don't stab the part so hard that the knife damages the part.

29

With so many small parts, bare plastic is inevitable. A delicate touch and a small brush are all you need to fix the problem.

regarding the photoetched metal at all.) So I had to measure the areas where the railing would go before cutting and bending. Dividers or calipers would work well, but I used a simple metal ruler, **31**.

To cut the railings from the continuous lengths on the fret, I placed it on a sheet of glass and pressed a sharp knife against the part, **32**. I used a pair of smooth-jawed pliers to bend the railings. I dipped the edge in a shallow pool of

super glue and placed the short railing with tweezers. For long railings, such as those that run along the main decks, I held them in position with automotive masking tape, **33**, which you can find at auto supply stores (look for a lower tack roll). Once a railing is in place, apply thin super glue to the join, **34**.

Automotive masking tape is used to tack the railing in place rather than another type of tape because accelerator

applied to the join between the deck and railing will set the super glue and dissolve the tape's adhesive, so the tape can be removed without damaging the paint or railing, **35**. This technique is easy to use and is great when you need to install railings with a gentle curve like the foredeck on the USS Cole, **36**.

Some paint is bound to come off the photoetched-metal railings while being handled, bent, and attached to the

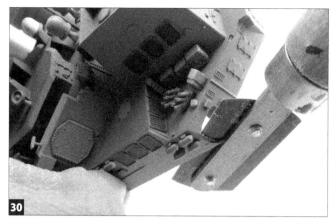

30 I sawed the join at the rear of the port side and spread it slightly to improve the fit of the side with the hull.

31 A ruler works well to measure easy-to-reach spots. If you are installing railings on busy superstructures, try dividers or calipers.

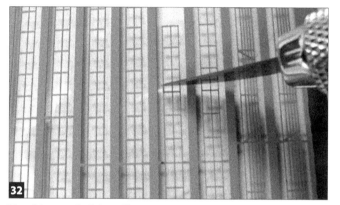

32 The thin metal of the railings is easily severed with a sharp knife blade pressed against a hard surface like glass.

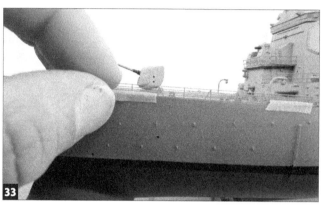

33 I used thin strips of automotive masking tape to hold the bow railings in place on the *Cole*. There's no glue involved at this point.

34 Thin super glue is pulled along the join between the railing and deck.

35 I lifted the tape edge with a knife blade and then gently pulled it off after softening the adhesive with super glue accelerant.

model. I touched up by running the side of a flat brush with neutral gray paint over the spots, **37**.

Decals. A quick note before I start: it a good idea to apply the decals before adding the bulk of the photoetched metal to minimize damage. I didn't, and I knocked several details off during the process.

The bulk of the model was painted in flat paint, which is not conducive to good decal adhesion. I could have sprayed the model with clear gloss, but there aren't that many decals and most are small. I decided to employ an easy-to-use alternative: Pledge Future floor polish. Yes, floor polish. Future is actually a hard-wearing, high-gloss clear acrylic that makes a perfect gloss coat. It can be air-

brushed, but it works well brush-painted too, which is how I used it to help apply decals to flat paint.

After dipping the decal in water, I painted Future over the area where the decal was to be applied, **38**. Then I floated the decal into the still-wet Future, **39**. To remove the excessive Future, I rolled a cotton swab over the surface, **40**. I brushed on another layer

36 I didn't bend the railing at the bow. The tape held it in position long enough for super glue to secure it on the deck.

37 To cover bare brass revealed by paint chipped off during handling, I brushed neutral gray over the affected areas.

38 I applied a layer of Pledge Future floor polish to the front deck in preparation for a large square decal to come.

39 Then I slid the decal into place in the pool of Future.

40 Carefully remove excess Future. Don't press hard or pull the decal because it will be hard to move around after the Future is gone.

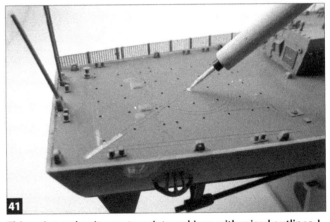

41 Thin paint makes it easy to paint markings with raised outlines. I flowed it into with a fine brush and let it run along the ridges.

of Future to seal the decals and help them conform. Most of the *Cole*'s decals went on well, but the large helicopter pad marking on the stern tore when I applied it. I painted on the markings instead, starting by flowing thin Tamiya flat white acrylic paint into the raised outline, **41**. I followed with progressively heavier layers of white until it looked right.

Rigging. Sailing ships abound with rigging, but even modern naval vessels have lines on masts and radio antennas. On *Arleigh Burke*-class destroyers, several lines hang from the main mast. During final assembly, I left the mast off. Using the kit's painting instructions, I drilled tiny holes in the mast's cross members with a pin vise, **42**. You can use stretched sprue or thread for

rigging, but I prefer invisible or nylon thread, actually very fine monofilament. I cut several pieces longer than necessary. After dipping one end in thick super glue, I threaded the lines into the holes, **43**. I glued the mast to the superstructure and threaded the loose ends through single holes at the base of each leg with tweezers, **44**, and trimmed off the excess with a sharp No. 11 blade.

42 The first step of installing rigging is drilling holes through the mast arms.

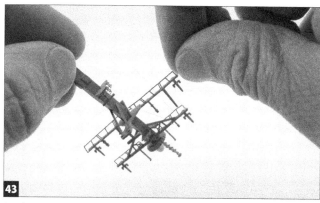

43 It takes a good eye to hit the tiny holes with the fine thread, but once they are in, the thick glue holds them in place as it sets.

44 A little eye strain is necessary to anchor the rigging into holes at the base of the mast, but a steady hand and tweezers do the trick.

45 I neatened things up by shaving the extra thread off the mast with a new blade.

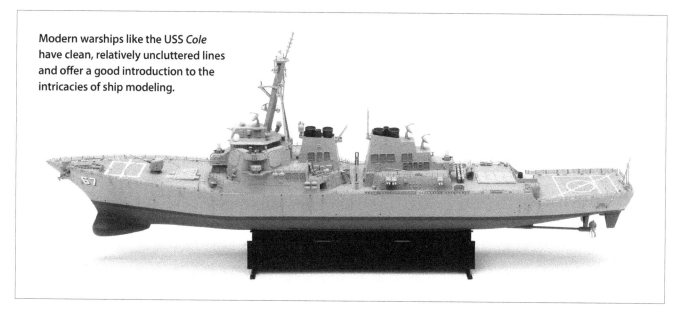

Modern warships like the USS *Cole* have clean, relatively uncluttered lines and offer a good introduction to the intricacies of ship modeling.

Maritime weathering. Several light coats of clear flat evened out the finish and eliminated glossy spots left by the Future and super glue. Weathering small scale ships presents challenges. It's easy to overdo it and make a well-maintained navy vessel look like a derelict rust bucket. Most are not, but they will show signs of use especially after a long deployment.

I added dark gray water streaks from the anchor hawsers and deck drains with pastels. Keep it light and subtle. I didn't apply washes and dry-brushing because I felt the contrast created would look unrealistic. Rust may seem logical, given the saltwater environment ships operate in, but it's best if used sparingly or avoided entirely.

Now all the *Cole* needs is a base for displaying it at sea.

7

Tackling
WEATHERING

Skills

- Handling photoetched metal
- Silly Putty masking
- Hairspray weathering
- Using pastels and pigments
- Making mud
- Post-shading

Weathering is a catch-all term for techniques applied to a model that enhance realism, giving it a worn appearance and a sense of how, when, and where the represented vehicle was used. Weathering includes techniques for highlighting detail, such as washes and dry-brushing, as well as extremes such as paint chipping, battle damage, and mud.

Weathering can be applied to any subject, even cars and airliners, but military vehicles benefit most from the extremes. I'll touch on recent advances in armor finishing techniques as well as old standbys as I build Dragon's 1/35 scale early production Tiger I Ausf E. Weathering is an art. Experiment with these and other techniques to expand your finishes.

1 Dragon's Tiger I is a plastic tour de force including photoetched-metal details and markings for three Leningrad front tanks.

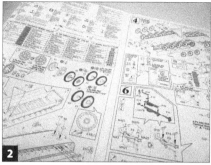

2 Highlighting the relevant steps in the instructions is a great way to avoid confusion between versions.

3 I highlighted the sprue designations with a marker to make finding parts easier.

4 Clear periscopes are nice details. To mask them before painting, place strips of Tamiya tape with a hobby knife.

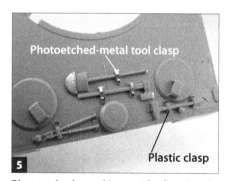

Photoetched-metal tool clasp

Plastic clasp

5 Photoetched metal is great for fine detail, but it can be frustrating. I used some of the clasps and other photoetched-metal parts to enhance the molded plastic tools.

6 I used the tip of a new No. 11 blade to maneuver small parts such as headlight bases into position. You don't have to press hard, just enough to pick up the piece.

The kit. Dragon kits are a tour de force among armor models. This Tiger, part of Dragon's Smart Kit range (No. 6600), includes photoetched-metal details, wire tow cables, and decals for three tanks operated by Germany's 502 Heavy Panzer Regiment on the Leningrad front in the winter of 1942–43, **1**. There are optional parts for the three versions that the complicated instructions point out. After deciding to build tank 100, I marked the optional parts I needed to be sure I didn't miss anything, **2**. There are 15 sprues in the box. To make finding needed parts

easier, I highlighted the sprues' letter tabs with a marker, **3**.

A few armor tips. The focus of this chapter is weathering, but here are a few tips for dealing with detailed armor models. Because I airbrushed the Tiger as opposed to spray-painting (as I did to the KV in Chapter 1), I attached the road-wheel arms and other suspension components at the start of the build. I left the overlapping road wheels off to be sure they all received paint.

Dragon provides clear periscopes, so I placed tiny strips of masking tape on

TIGER TANK

Armed with a powerful 88mm gun and protected by as much as 100mm of armor, German Tiger tanks presented the Allies with a thorny opponent. Design work for a heavy tank began in 1937, and the first vehicle entered service in August 1942. The first combat occurred the following month with the 502nd Tank Battalion near Leningrad. Although changes

This Tiger tank was captured in Tunisia. *U.S. Army photo*

were made to the engine, road wheels, and commander's cupola during production, the basic design stayed essentially the same for the more than 1,340 Tiger Is built.

Tigers served in North Africa, Russia, and northwest Europe and proved deadly for many Allied tanks, although the vehicle was not without it's problems, especially mechanical deficiencies that sidelined many. However, Tigers have become an iconic tank and are wildly popular modeling subjects. Tank 100 of the 502nd battalion modeled here is noteworthy as the first Tiger captured intact by the Soviets in January 1943.

the areas to remain clear before adding the covers, **4**.

The kit offers a comprehensive set of photoetched-metal parts including tool clasps, straps, and brackets; engine frames; and other details (some with optional plastic parts). Pick and choose the parts you use—just because there are photoetched-metal parts provided doesn't mean you have to use them, **5**.

Lots of detail means lots of small parts. After applying a little liquid cement to the mounting locations, I moved small parts with the tip of a new No. 11 blade, **6**. For very small parts, leave a little handle of sprue attached to make them easier to handle, **7**. You can trim the handle off after the glue dries, **8**.

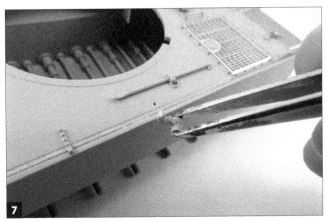

7 I left a little bit of sprue attached to a tow-cable bracket to provide the tweezers with a better grip.

8 Sprue cutters make quick work of the sprue handle once the glue is dry.

9 Hold the knife flat against the surface as you shave the casting numbers from the sprue. Work slowly, rocking the knife slightly to cut the plastic without damaging the number.

10 To fill an unexpected gap on the hull, I slid a styrene-strip shim into the space. Liquid cement will secure it, and sanding will make it invisible under paint.

11 Ready for paint. In addition to the wheels, the only parts I left off until after painting were the smoke dischargers. The photoetched metal parts and wire tow cables are obvious in this photo.

12 Don't throw away cardboard; it makes a great small-parts holder during painting. I used poster putty to hold the wheels.

The Tiger includes tiny numbers molded on a sprue to replicate the casting number on the mantlet. You can also use part numbers for this purpose. Simply shave the number off with a sharp blade, **9**, and place it on the model by flooding it with liquid cement.

After attaching the upper hull, I noticed it was short a fraction of an inch. I filled the gap by inserting a strip of .030" styrene and flowing in liquid cement, **10**.

There are two schools of thought when it comes to tools, tow cables, and other details mounted on the hull. Some modelers prefer to paint all of them off the model and attach them at the end of the build. I prefer to attach them during construction and paint them on the model after airbrushing the camouflage. This allows the glue to work without having to scrape paint and minimizes damage to the finish from adhesive.

13 I primed the tank with flat black enamel. It hides the differences between materials (metal and plastic), reveals surface flaws, and adds depth to the finish.

14 Having found a blob of dry glue, I sanded it away.

15 This is the initial primer coat, so don't be bashful when sanding blemishes. Now is the time to get rid of them, and the next coat of primer will cover the plastic.

16 The smoother the primer, the better the finish. I rubbed the entire model with 1000-grit sandpaper to remove rough spots.

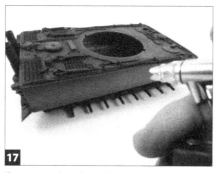

17 Start spraying the schwarzgrau base coat at the center of the panels and work out so a hint of the black primer is visible.

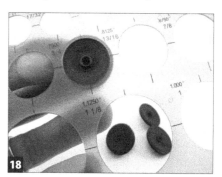

18 Painting road wheels can be a chore, but using a circle template helps. Just find the hole size that covers the tire but leaves the wheel exposed.

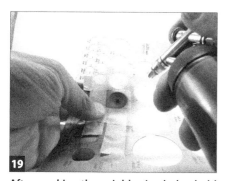

19 After masking the neighboring holes, hold each wheel up to the hole and airbrush away. It took me about 15 minutes to paint all 30 of the Tiger's road wheels.

20 Airbrush the lighter shade onto the panel's center and feather it out. It doesn't have to be perfect.

21 Post-shading is a great way to make a monochromatic finish look more dynamic. It also works on aircraft and other models.

It does take a steady hand, however. The model is now ready for painting, **11**.

Prime it black. In preparation for painting, I mounted the road wheels on a piece of cardboard with poster putty, **12**. Although in most cases, primer is light gray or white, I like to prime armor with black or dark brown, **13**. Not only does the dark color blend the entire surface together for the paint, but it also adds depth to the finish. Take your time during this phase of finish-

ing. If you get the dark color in recesses and behind overhangs, it will serve as shadows on the finished model.

The primer revealed a couple of glue spots, so I gently sanded them, **14**, until the area was all smooth, **15**. Then, I lightly sanded the model with 1000-grit sandpaper, **16**. This step may seem unnecessary, but keeping the paint smooth between each coat prevents buildup. You don't need to press hard; a light touch is all that's needed to knock any rough spots

off the surface. Once I was satisfied, I sprayed another coat of black.

Camouflage. I loaded my airbrush with an equal mix of Model Master panzer schwarzgrau enamel and Model Master enamel thinner and set the needle to a medium-wide spray pattern. I airbrushed the model starting at the middle of panels and working out so a shadow of the black remained, **17**. You don't need to lay on the paint to get gray under every nook,

22

In addition to making the model shiny, hairspray seals the paint and makes the acrylic whitewash easy to remove.

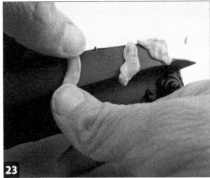

23

Silly Putty, serious masking: to recreate the Tiger's unique winter camo, I pressed the sticky putty to the hull and turret.

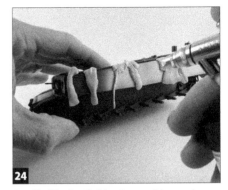

24

Applied in the field, winter whitewash was a thin paint that tended to wear quickly, so I varied the density as I airbrushed Tamiya white.

25

This view shows the patchy white paint to good effect.

26

Starting on the glacis plate, I scrubbed the white paint from the Tiger. I tried to imagine the areas of the vehicle that would suffer the most wear and tear.

27

A small brush with the bristle cut to about ⅛" is the perfect tool for fine work on edges and corners.

cranny, or tool because the black primer naturally adds shadows.

Painting the road wheels takes a little more preparation. The black primer will work for the rubber tires, so preserving it is a good idea, but that means masking each of the 30 road wheels or brush-painting them. This is where a circle template comes in handy. Look for them at artist supply stores and pick a plastic one that has several holes sizes. After determining which cutout masked the tire best, **18**, I taped over the surrounding holes to prevent overspray. Then it was a simple matter of centering each wheel behind the cutout and spraying them gray, **19**. Because I was using enamels, I left the paint to dry for several days between each layer.

Post-shading. This step was probably not essential on this whitewashed Tiger, but I use it on most of my armor and some aircraft, especially those with monochromatic finishes. Varying the tone of the main color breaks up the finish and makes the model visually dynamic.

To start, lighten the base color. I find that white tends to make certain colors appear chalky when added to lighten them, so I prefer to use a similar color such as yellow or tan with dark green, light or sky blue with dark blues, and, as in this case, camouflage gray with schwarzgrau. You don't want too stark a contrast so add a little of the lighter color at a time and mix as you go. Then mix in a little more thinner than normal. This gives you more control over the density of the shade. Mixing in a little clear will do the same thing.

I set the airbrush to a narrow pattern and sprayed panel centers, feathering the effect toward the edges, **20**. Don't spray all the way to the panel edges, but you don't have to keep it perfectly neat either. The idea is to break up the base coat. You can lighten the mix a little more and concentrate on the very center of the panels for more variation. Or instead of panel centers, airbrush one side of the panels, using an index card or other mask to keep the edge crisp. Whichever method you use, post-shading should produce an interesting vehicle, **21**.

Hairspray (really). The crucial element of recreating realistically distressed winter whitewash is not a scale modeling product but rather one you might find human models using—hairspray. Based on the work of FSM author Karl Logan, I used Aqua Net Extra Super Hold, but I suspect most common hairsprays will work, **22**. Test it first on a spare part or bit of styrene painted with the same paint being used on the model.

I gave the Tiger two coats of hairspray. It comes out of the can fast so keep the nozzle moving. Don't worry if it pools a little or has an orange-peel texture while wet; as it dries, it leaves the model smooth and slightly glossy. Don't forget the road wheels. I only sprayed the outer faces of the first two rows of wheels, the ones visible from the outside. After spraying, put the model aside to dry for two days.

Whitewash. The Tigers of the 502nd wore a unique splotchy whitewash. I masked it with Silly Putty, pulling and stretching

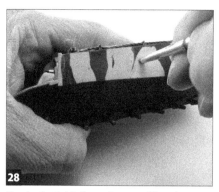

28 On the hull, I followed natural brush strokes to wear the paint. I chipped the lower edge where dirt and rocks from the tracks would likely strike the paint.

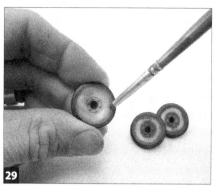

29 The small brush made quick work of the road wheels. I concentrated on removing white paint from the center and rim.

30 A thin coat of Tamiya clear orange over brown makes the tool handles look like varnished wood.

31 Alignment of the wheels is critical so double-check each one against the others and the hull as you attach them.

32 I blended the finish and emphasized recessed detail first with an overall wash of dark brown artist's oil.

33 Pinwashes, targeted applications of thin artist's oils, deepen shadows such as weld seams. Touch a pointed brush to the detail and let capillary action do the rest.

34 To corrode the Tiger's big exhausts, I painted them with Model Master rust, a dark red-brown enamel.

35 I held a brush of talcum powder over the wet paint and flicked and tapped it to deposit a little at a time.

36 The sprinkling of baby powder gives the pipes a lightly pitted texture as the paint dries.

rolled worms onto the turret and hull to match the painting diagram, **23**. Silly Putty is great for this because it sticks well enough to work as a temporary mask, it comes off readily when you need it to, and it is easily pushed and prodded into any shape. The only downside is that it tends to flow as it sits on the surface and the masks can shift slightly, so you have to work quickly.

The most important part of the next step is to use acrylic paint. If you use

enamels, you won't be able to rub the paint off with a wet brush, defeating the whole process. I mixed Tamiya white and thinner 50:50, set the nozzle to a relatively narrow pattern, and dialed the pressure down to about 15 psi. I sprayed the whitewash in a patchy pattern—thin in some spots, denser in other—and moved the brush in the direction I imagined the crew in the field would have, **24** and **25**. I set the model aside to dry for about an hour.

Whitewash removal. To weather the whitewash, I filled a small container with water and found a couple of old, stiff brushes: a flat one and an old round brush with the bristles trimmed to about ⅛".

I dipped the flat brush into the water, blotted off the excess water, and rubbed the brush over the model where I wanted to remove the whitewash, **26**. You may need to apply a little pressure to start eroding the acrylic paint but be careful not to scratch the surface with

WORKING WITH PHOTOETCHED METAL

Photoetched metal is thin steel or brass onto which shapes are transferred through a photographic process and then etched. The parts are thin, can be easily bent, and do a great job of representing metal. The material used to be primarily an aftermarket item, but it is now widely included in kits of every genre, so it's important to be comfortable using it. Whether aftermarket or kit-supplied, brass or steel, the techniques for handling and attaching photoetched metal are the same.

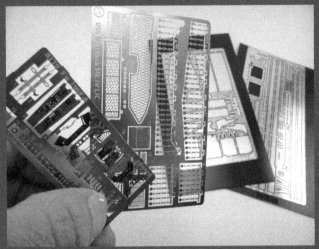

Here are a few examples of photoetched metal, including a set from an Academy kit, an aftermarket set from Griffon, and a fret of color parts from Eduard. Some parts are even self-adhesive to make application easier.

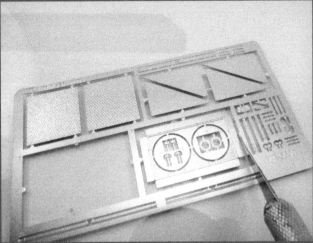

Most parts are attached to the fret with minute points. The simplest way to remove them is with a sharp hobby knife. Place the fret on a hard surface such as glass or tile and pull the knife across the attachment point as close to the part as possible.

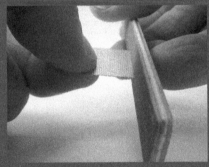

To remove the tiny metal tab left after the part is removed, hold the part against a fine sanding stick or honing stone and drag it against the abrasive in the direction of the edge, not across it.

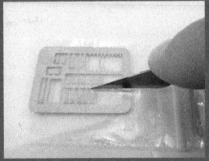

When removing photoetched parts with a knife, it's easy to launch parts into stratosphere. To avoid crawling around looking for a sliver of brass, place the fret inside a zipper-close bag. Then cut through the bag to remove the part.

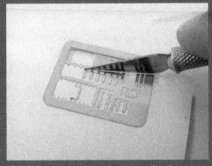

Another solution is to press the fret onto the sticky strip of a Post-it note before cutting the part from the fret. The adhesive is tacky enough to hold onto the part.

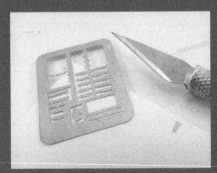

After cutting the part away, peel the fret from the Post-it note. Then flex the Post-it note and poke the tip of a hobby knife under an edge and remove the piece.

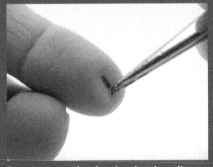

Tweezers may be the simplest bending tools, especially for small parts. Hold the part with tweezers near a bend point and press it against the fleshy part of a finger.

Smooth-jawed pliers are useful for larger bends. They hold the part and give you a straight edge to bend the metal against without marring the surface.

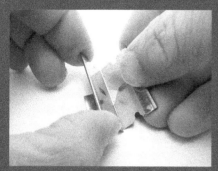

For larger parts, use two single-edge razor blades. Hold one blade along the fold point. Then slide the other blade under the part and pivot the metal piece up.

For very long bends, use a tool such as a Mission Models Etch Mate, the Hold and Fold from The Small Shop, or benders sold by UMM-USA. They clamp the metal in place and provide a sturdy surface to bend the metal against.

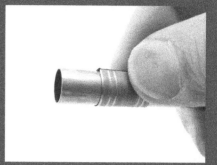

For curves, cylinders, or cones, look for a similarly sized item such a brass rod or wire that you can use as a mandrel.

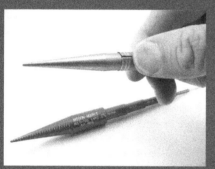

Tools such as Mission Models Multi-Tools or the Rollmade Universal Roller from UMM-USA work as well.

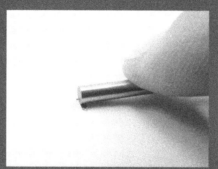

For small parts that need just a gentle curve, roll a cylinder back and forth over the part several times. The more you do this, the more the part will curl.

Metal is naturally springy, which can make bending it difficult. To lessen the springiness, briefly heat the part over a candle flame.

Then let the part cool slowly to room temperature.

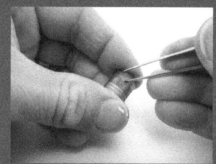

Now you should be able to bend, crumple, or crinkle the part. This is a great way to add battle damage to tank fenders.

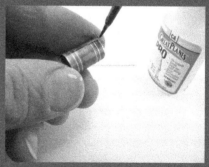

Super glue is the most common adhesive for attaching metal parts. I usually use a thicker cement because the natural tackiness holds the part in position as the glue sets.

37. Touch a brush damp with a thin light rust color to the dry paint/talcum powder mix. It'll soak in and color the white powder.

38. To give the tracks a warm steel look, I airbrushed them with a mix of Tamiya brown and metallic gray.

39. Tank tracks usually have a layer of old rust. I applied a wash of red-brown artist's oils. Using less thinner than normal for a wash allows the paint to cover better.

40. A thin black wash deepens the shadows.

41. Finally, dry-brushing the tracks with metallic gray gives the high points the appearance of bare metal, as if contact with the ground kept the areas rust free.

42. I added a film of dirt by airbrushing a thin mix of brown paint and clear flat over the lower hull and running gear.

the ferule (the metal part that holds the bristles).

I used the small brush to get into tight corners as well as to remove the paint from hatches and edges, **27**. I tried to wear the paint in areas it would most likely be worn by the crew—around hatches, the glacis plate, and engine deck—or damaged by use—edges, corners, and fenders, **28**. On the road wheels, I concentrated on the centers, removing paint from the bolts and the rims, **29**. Work carefully but quickly—the longer the paint has been on the model, the harder it is to remove.

Tools, wheels, and decals. I painted the tools with a 5/0 brush. The metal head on the shovel, hammer, axe, and hammer, as well as the pry bars are Tamiya black. The wire cutters are Tamiya metallic black. For the tool handles, cleaning rod, and the jack block, I applied Vallejo new wood and streaked Vallejo weathered wood to give the impression of grain. Then, I applied thin Tamiya clear orange to the handles but not to the block; once the paint was dry, the handles looked like varnished wood, **30**. I

painted the tow cables and spare track links metallic gray and applied a light rust wash.

I didn't use clear gloss before adding the decals (there are only a few markings) relying on multiple applications of Micro Sol to settle the decals over the flat paint.

Next came the wheels. Pay attention to the instructions to be sure you get the road wheels in the right order and constantly check alignment, **31**. To accent panel lines and other recessed detail, I applied an artist's oil wash, burnt umber and a little yellow ochre, **32**. Work with very thin paint to keep the effects subtle. If you want to emphasize a certain area, apply the wash directly to the recess with a fine-point brush, **33**.

After a few days, I airbrushed the model with Model Master Acryl clear flat to cut the sheen left by the hairspray, gloss white, and artist's oils and to tie the model together.

Exhausts and tracks. I brush-painted the Tiger's prominent exhausts Model master rust enamel, **34**. While the paint was wet, I tapped talcum powder onto the pipes

to create a lightly pitted texture, typical of the corrosion hot metal develops when exposed to wet weather, **35** and **36**. Finally, I mixed a thin light rust color from artist's oils. The wash soaked into the powder, eliminated the white, and varied the color a little, **37**.

Dragon Styrene (DS) tracks are great; they are flexible like vinyl tracks, but they can be colored with normal model paint and glued with styrene cement. I basecoated the Tiger's big tracks with Tamiya metallic gray mixed with a little brown to produce a warm steel color, **38**. Then I applied a wash, slightly thicker than usual, of 502 Abteilung rust-colored artist's oil, taking time to be sure it reached every recess, **39**. A final wash of thin lamp black oil paint deepened the shadows, **40**. To show bare metal where the links make contact with the ground, I dry-brushed Tamiya metallic gray, **41**.

Getting dirty. The first step I take when weathering any vehicle is to airbrush a layer of dust over its lower areas. For the Tiger, I tinted thin Model Master Acryl

43 Vary the density of the dirt by concentrating the paint in certain areas and spraying vertical streaks up the hull.

44 Mud pie anybody? Here's the recipe for mud: plaster, pigments or pastels for color, acrylic gel medium, and water. You can also add dirt for texture.

45 Combine the pigments and plaster to match the mud to the battlefield that you are modeling.

46 Stir water and acrylic gel medium into the dry ingredients. If it's too thick, add gel medium; more plaster will thicken the mix.

47 Use an old brush to spread the mud. You'll probably want to throw it out after this weathering session.

48 Think about where mud will get thrown by the tracks: under fenders, on hull sides and wheels, and on the front and rear, especially near idlers and drive sprockets.

49 Tank crews climb over the vehicle to get in and out. I tracked a little mud over the hull front, engine deck, and turret.

50 Applying more than one shade of mud spices up the weathering.

51 Don't forget to add mud and dirt to the tracks. Working it into each link is time consuming but the effect is worth the effort.

WEATHERING PRINCIPLES

Weathering is one of the most subjective aspects of modeling. Show six modelers the same model, and you'll likely get six opinions ranging from "it's not dirty enough" to "it would never run with that much mud" or "not enough rust." I enjoy weathering because I think it's a great way to communicate how, when, and where the vehicle was used. Here are a few basic principles that work for me:

Keep it subtle. The dirt, dust, and mud should be like it was deposited by use, not by the hand of God. If I can see how you did it, it's probably too much. Err on the side of less, and remember, you can always add more later.

Research the vehicle you are modeling. Match the weathering to the time and place you want to represent. Not all weathering techniques are appropriate on every model. For example, a British 8th Army Matilda in the North African theater probably wouldn't have a lot of mud caked up under the fenders. On the other hand, the Tiger I built was used on the Leningrad front in the winter of 1942–43, so mud and caked dirt seemed natural. Also, consider how long the vehicle has been in service.

Use photos when possible. Looking at photos of vehicles in the theater or area you are modeling will show you appropriate areas of wear and tear.

Think in terms of layers. In the real world, dirt gets built up over time. Think about weathering the same way and apply weathering in layers, rather than trying to add everything at once.

52
My thumb proved useful in removing mud from the track high points and forcing the mixture into the treads.

53
The vinyl tracks need to remain flexible. As the mud dried, I flexed and bent the tracks. Some of the mud chipped and dropped out, adding the effect of old mud embedded in the links.

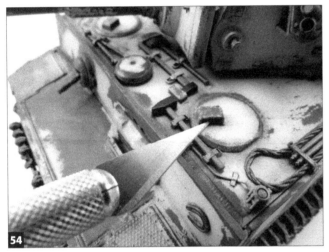

54
Painting done, I removed the masks from the periscopes with a hobby knife.

55
Use pigments from a palette rather than directly from the bottle to avoid contaminating it with other colors or moisture.

clear flat with a few drops of Model Master Acryl wood. I airbrushed this behind the suspension and under the fenders as well as along the lower edge of the hull sides and around the front and back using a narrow spray pattern and pressure of 12–15 psi, **42**. I built up the density on the lower hull but kept it thin higher up. To vary the look, I airbrushed a few vertical streaks up the hull sides, **43**. Around the hull front, I concentrated the dust around the tracks. I applied the tinted clear heavily around the vehicle's rear panel, especially around the tracks.

Playing in the mud. Mud can be represented in several ways (I've used Celluclay and putty), but for the Tiger, I used acrylic gel medium and plaster mixed with dirt. You can find gel medium at art supply stores; for this project, I used Mig Produc-

tions medium as well as Mig's powdered pigments for color, **44**. I mixed the plaster powder with a little Mig dry mud and light European earth, **45**, and then added water and acrylic gel medium and stirred until it reached a consistency of thick mud, **46**. A little soil from my yard added texture. Using an old, stiff brush, I glopped the mud behind the running gear and under the fenders, **47**. I also ran some around the rim of the road wheels.

This early Tiger doesn't have the fender extensions common on later versions, so the tracks extend past the hull, and I figured mud would be deposited along the hull sides, **48**. The front hull, especially around the spare tracks and the drive sprockets, got a healthy dose of mud. I threw a lot of mud at the back of the hull, imagining where the big tracks would deposit it. I even applied a little to the

turret top and glacis plate as if crew men had tracked it there, **49**. I mixed a darker shade of mud and painted splotches of it over the other mud to add a little variety, **50**. Tank tracks churn up the earth, so a lot of it collects in the treads. I slopped mud into the tracks, **51**, and used a finger to remove it from high points, **52**. As it dried, I bent and flexed the tracks to separate the mud from the links, **53**.

Tracks and pigments. Once the mud was dry, I attached the track. The great thing about DS tracks is that they can be glued with solvent cement. After wrapping them around the running gear, I sanded paint from the top of a few of the road wheels, so I could glue the tracks to them. This gives the top run the Tiger's distinctive front-high appearance. Paintbrush handles held the tracks in place as the super

56

I applied Mig soot pigment to the exhaust pipes to show the output from the big diesel power plant.

57

If you get powdered pigments on areas you don't want and blowing is not enough to remove it, rub a finger across the area.

58

I let Mig's pigment fixer soak into the pigments to secure them to the pipes.

59

All the work I did on the track obscured some of the high points and rubbed the paint off others. I repainted them with Tamiya metallic gray to finish the Tiger.

glue set. I removed the masking tape from the periscopes with the tip of knife, **54**.

I used Mig pigments to finish the weathering, but artist's pastel chalks work just as well. I like the pigments for the convenience and location- and condition-specific colors, **55**. Pigments and pastels are best applied with a soft brush. Pick a little up on the bristles and then brush or flick them over the area to be weathered, **56**. Use a light touch and blow the excess off; the powder is easily feathered and controlled. In addition to soot on the exhaust pipes, I added a little extra dust and dirt to the corners on the hull, **57**. Mig makes a pigment fixer, a great way to make sure the powder doesn't go walkabout, **58**. You can also use turpentine, alcohol, and water to create different effects. As a final touch, I painted the high points of the tracks Tamiya metallic gray, and the Tiger was done, **59**.

The Russian winter was hard on men and machines. Appropriate weathering applied well can communicate that and much more about this Eastern Front Tiger I.

8

IMPROVING
an Older Kit

Skills

- Working with resin parts
- Using white metal
- Scribing panel lines
- Airbrushing metal finishes

F-80 Shooting Star

MONOGRAM

1/48 Scale / Escala / Échelle • Ages 10 & Up / Edades 10 y mas / À partir de 10 ans

Modern kits are masterpieces of molding and detail. Some are so well made that filler and sanding are rarely needed, and construction can take a few short hours, allowing the builder to focus on painting and finishing. There are times when you want to build an older kit, either because it may be the only model of the subject or because you have the kit in your stash.

The Monogram 1/48 scale F-80 Shooting Star is a good example of the former. Recently reissued by Revell, the kit debuted in 1977, but it's still the only option if you want a 1/48 scale model of this Korean War combatant.

1 Raised panel lines were once the only option, but most modelers don't like them because they lack realism and don't take weathering washes.

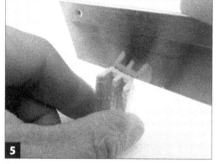

3 Westley's Bleche-Wite is a strong tire cleaner that will break up oily mold-release agents. Wear gloves if you have to get your hands in the solution, for example, when you are removing the parts.

5 Sawing is the best way to remove pour plugs. You can cut slowly and check your work often to prevent mistakes.

2 The detail in Monogram's plastic cockpit tub isn't bad, but the True Details resin tub is more refined and has lots of knobs and switches that are not on the kit's cockpit.

4 Pour plugs are excess resin usually left where the liquid resin was poured into the mold. Most manufacturers put them in easy-to-hide locations like the bottom of the F-80 ejection seat.

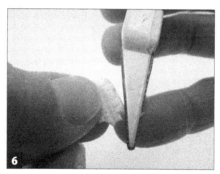

6 I used a sander to remove excess resin in the instrument panel. Always check instructions before cutting or sanding, so you don't remove something important.

It's not a bad kit: the shapes are good, and it goes together okay. The detail in the cockpit is passable, but the surface is marked with raised panel lines, **1**. They were standard on model kits until the 1980s when engraved panel lines became vogue. When I built the reissue recently, I decided to replace the raised lines by re-scribing them and finish the model with a shiny natural-metal skin. While I was at it, I added a resin cockpit, **2**, wheels, and Misawa wingtip fuel tanks.

What is resin? Speaking technically, ure-thane resin is the product of a two-part material that can be poured into a mold to cast parts. For modelers, this results in having more detailed parts than those made of injection-molded styrene. These very detailed parts can really improve the appearance of models. Like photoetched

LOCKHEED F-80 SHOOTING STAR

Originally designated the P-80, Lockheed's Shooting Star became the U.S. Air Force's first operational jet fighter when it entered service in late 1944. Too late to see combat in World War II, the single-engine airplane rose to prominence in the early months of the Korean War when it was the only USAF jet in the theater. Despite some success in air-to-air combat, the F-80 was outmatched by the swept-wing MiG-15 and was transformed into a potent ground-attack aircraft.

Shooting Stars from the 8th Fighter-Bomber Squadron fly over Korea.
U.S. Air Force photo

Armed with six .50-caliber machine guns in the nose, the F-80C could carry rockets, bombs, and napalm canisters. The RF-80 reconnaissance version exchanged guns for cameras. By mid-1951, most F-80s had been withdrawn from frontline service, but the basic design soldiered on for many years as the two-seat T-33 trainer. Several are still flying with the Bolivian Air Force, and Boeing used one as a chase plane during flight tests of the 787 Dreamliner in 2010.

metal, resin parts used to be the province of aftermarket manufacturers, but more and more kits from major manufacturers are including resin, especially for cockpits and wheel wells.

Unfortunately, all that detail doesn't come without negatives. Resin tends to be more fragile, so care must be taken during handling. There are also occasional molding problems, including air bubbles and warping. And because the parts are not plastic, they usually need more test-fitting and refinement before they can be installed.

Resin preparation. Cleaning plastic parts before painting is a good idea, but it's essential for resin parts. Most have a strong mold-release agent that will repel

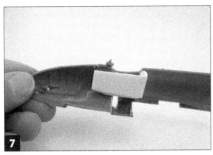

7

Although the cockpit set was designed to be used with the Monogram kit, the parts needed work to fit. The tub sat too high in front because of the nose wheel well.

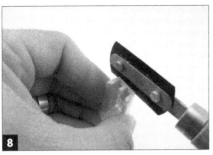

8

I used a small saw to cut a chunk from the floor of the cockpit to get a better fit.

9

Maintain even pressure when sanding the backing from flat resin items and check your progress frequently.

10

I used thick super glue to attach most resin parts. The extended setting time allows you to position the part, and the gel fills minor gaps.

11

I brush-painted the resin cockpit with a mix of Model Master and Tamiya acrylics.

12

I squished lead sinkers to fit the tight spaces in the F-80's nose to help keep all three wheels on the ground.

13

Hearing lead weights rolling around inside the fuselage is disturbing. Using epoxy is messy, but it secures the sinkers.

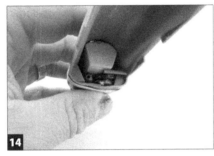

14

I added more sinkers under the cockpit to make sure the plane stays grounded.

15

Available from office supply stores, Dymo lettering tape is sturdy, self-adhesive, and flexible, making it an ideal scribing guide.

paint. You can scrub the parts with dishwashing detergent and an old toothbrush, but I prefer to soak the parts overnight in Westley's Bleche-Wite tire cleaner, agitating the container periodically, **3**. The next day, I rinse the parts in clear water and let them air dry.

Most resin parts come attached to a pour stub that will need to be removed, **4**. The excess is usually obvious, but check the instructions as a reference to make sure you don't chop off an essential part. It's possible to use sprue cutters to remove the blocks, but I prefer a razor saw, **5**. Using a saw allows you to work slowly, cut close to the part, and check

your progress to avoid mistakes. Cut gently to prevent breakage. (Wear a respirator and eye protection when sawing or sanding resin; the dust is irritating and can be harmful.) I refine the cut surface with a sanding stick, **6**.

Sometimes you'll need to remove more than just the pour stub so the part fits. When I test-fit the cockpit of the F-80, it was obviously too high at the front, where it hit the nose wheel well, **7**. I cut slivers of resin from under the cockpit, **8**, and dry-fit the part until it fit.

To remove the pour plug from flat parts, such as the side walls of the F-80, I placed a piece of sandpaper on a flat

surface. After placing the part, pour plug down, on the paper, I rubbed it in a circular motion and gradually eroded the plug, **9**. The excess resin will become paper thin and fall away, leaving just the part.

Gluing and painting resin. Super glue is the adhesive of choice for attaching resin to plastic or resin to resin. (Solvent-based model cement won't work at all.) I like to use thick super glue because the slower setting time gives you time to position a part, and it's tacky enough to hold the part in place as the glue sets, **10**.

If the parts have been properly cleaned, any model paint will work to

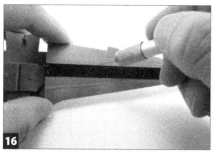

16 I dragged the needle's tip back and forth along the tape, removing a sliver of plastic each time and gradually engraving the panel line.

17 The point of a hobby knife also works as a scriber.

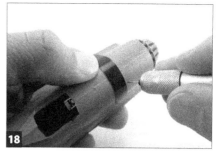

18 The self-adhesive labeling tape works well to guide the scriber around the fuselage.

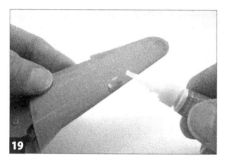

19 Make a mistake? To fix, first apply a little super glue over the misplaced line.

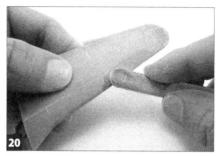

20 Next, sand the area smooth. Then you can scribe the correct line, even through the super glue.

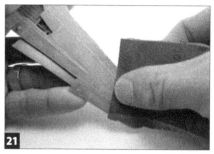

21 I sanded off the raised panel lines and smoothed the edges of the engraved panel lines.

color the resin. I used a combination of Model Master and Tamiya acrylics for the F-80 cockpit. I painted the floor, lower walls, and rear bulkhead interior green and the instrument panels flat black, **11**. I dry-brushed the panel with Panzer gray to highlight instruments and then painted other controls with silver, red, and yellow applied with a fine brush. The ejection-seat was black with khaki cushions, the head rest olive drab, and the harness off-white.

Nose weight. Shooting Stars have a lot of airplane behind the main wheels, so the model will end up a tail-sitter if weight isn't added to the front of the plane. Lead fishing sinkers work perfectly, but there isn't a lot of room in the nose because the kit includes detail of the gun bays. To get more in the tight space, I flattened several sinkers with a pair of locking pliers, **12**. To ensure none of them slipped loose after the fuselage was closed, I installed them with 5-minute epoxy, **13**. Concerned that I didn't have enough weight up front to keep the nose wheel down, I added more sinkers in the void under the cockpit, **14**.

Scribing panel lines. When engraving detail, it's important to keep the lines straight and even. You can use a metal straight edge or any one of several purpose-built scribing templates as a guide. But the easiest guide, especially for long panel lines, is thick self-adhesive labeling tape, commonly called Dymo tape, **15**. It stays in place, is flexible enough to go around fuselages and wings, and is thick enough to be the perfect scribing guide. I peeled the backing from a piece long enough to span one wing and then carefully stuck it to one of the wings with an edge aligned with a panel line.

I own several scribers with a variety of handle designs and blade dimensions, but the most useful tool is a sewing needle chucked in a pin vise. It's easy to use: lightly drag the needle's point along the edge of the tape several times, **16**. If you don't have a pin vise and needle handy, the back edge of a hobby knife will suffice, **17**. Dymo tape works well around fuselages, **18**, but for odd shapes or access panels, you may want to buy special templates.

Mistakes happen when scribers get a little off course or skip, but these mistakes are easy to fix. First, apply a little super

glue to the bad groove, **19**. Then set the glue with a little accelerator and sand smooth, **20**. I scribed the major components—front fuselage, rear fuselage, wing, and horizontal stabilizers—separately for ease of handling.

Once all the lines are scribed, I sanded the surfaces with 400-grit and then 1000-grit sandpaper to remove the raised panel lines and knock off any burrs left by the scriber, **21**. I cleared sanding debris and residue from the panel lines with the needle, **22**. Then, a couple of passes with a razor saw repaired panel lines across seams, **23**.

Resin wingtips. A late addition to my plans was adding larger Misawa fuel tanks. The resin set included not only the tanks but replacement wingtips with heavy-duty tank mounts. To replace, I started by sawing off the last ¼" of the wings, **24**. This was less than I needed to remove, but it's always better to cut too little and sand to refine the fit, instead of cutting away something you can't replace. I checked the fit, sanded, fit again, and sanded until the resin parts fit, **25**. Once I was satisfied with the fit, I attached the tips with thick super glue and sanded the join smooth, **26**. I left the tanks separate for painting.

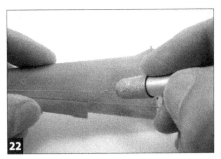

22 I removed debris from the panel lines with the needle.

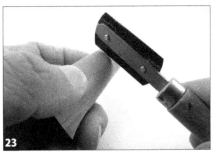

23 Saws make great scribers as well. They are especially useful for repairing lines lost when seams are sanded.

24 I clipped the Shooting Star's wings with a razor saw in preparation for mounting Misawa long-range fuel tanks.

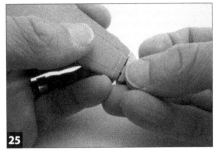

25 Measure twice and cut once are great words to live by. Always remove less material than necessary and then refine the shape with sanding.

26 Use thick super glue to attach the new tip to the wing. Sanding removed the bead of glue that oozed out of the join and also blended the parts.

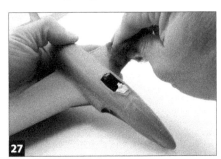

27 Steel wool may seem a little harsh, but it's a great tool for smoothing plastic in preparation for painting.

28 I used dish soap and an old, soft toothbrush to remove sanding debris and grease from the model to prepare it for painting.

29 I sprayed the model gloss black as a base coat for the Alclad II polished aluminum lacquer. The finish should be as smooth as possible.

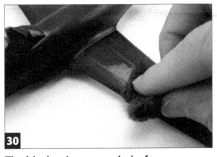

30 The black primer revealed a few surface inconsistencies. Don't worry about removing paint at this stage; there is at least one more primer layer to come.

Surface preparation. I planned to use Alclad II lacquer to give the Shooting Star a realistic natural-metal finish, but no matter what you use, the most important step is surface preparation. Metallic paints and foil are extremely thin and reveal any scratches or blemishes, so time spent getting the surface smooth is critical.

After using 600- and 1000-grit sandpaper, I buffed the plastic with OOOO steel wool in a circular pattern, **27**. All of the sanding and handling leaves the plastic covered in dust and skin oil. I cleaned the surface with a mild dish detergent mix, scrubbing engraved detail with an old,

soft toothbrush, **28**. I rinsed the model in cool, clear water and left it to air-dry for several hours. Don't rush into painting after washing because the surface may appear dry, but water collects in wheel wells and engine openings, and any water running out during painting will spoil the finish.

Alclad polished aluminum requires a gloss black base coat, so I sprayed the model with Tamiya black, **29**. Spray this as you would any gloss finish: start with a couple of mist coats and work up to heavy wet coats. Just like primer, the black revealed a few rough spots. I sanded the offending areas with 1000-grit paper and

OOOO steel wool, **30**, and then washed the surface to remove the debris before spraying more black. I had to repeat this process several times before the surface looked glass smooth.

Applying Alclad. I've used several metallic paints, but I like Alclad II for its versatility and strength. The lacquer is available in several shades of aluminum, **31**. It's designed to be airbrushed unthinned, but when you look at the bottle, it looks like it's about 95 percent clear with a tiny layer of metallic pigment at the bottom. Don't worry, the results will knock your socks off, and Alclad is very easy to use.

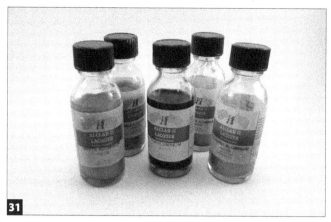

31 Alclad II natural-metal finishes come in several shades.

32 Alclad works best by layering. Mist the metallic lacquer over the model, gradually building up the paint and the shine. The mirror-like finish makes all of the surface preparation worthwhile.

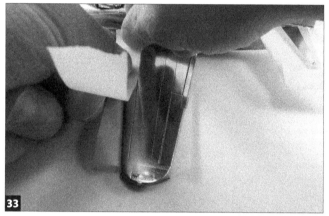

33 One of Alclad II's biggest advantages is the speed with which it dries. It can be masked and painted over within minutes. Use a low-tack tape for masking and don't burnish the tape too hard.

34 I sprayed duraluminum, which is darker than polished aluminum, over masked panels on the wings, stabilzers, and fuselage.

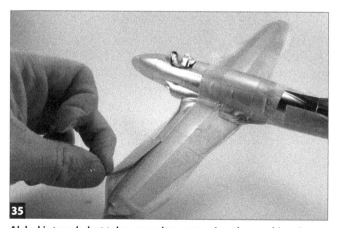

35 Alclad is tough, but take care when removing the masking. I peeled the tape back against itself.

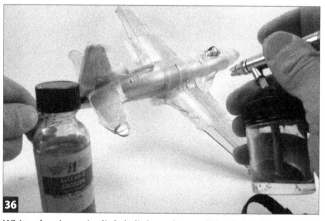

36 White aluminum is slightly lighter than polished aluminum, so it makes for good contrast on selected panels.

After shaking the lacquer bottle until all of the sediment is off the bottom, fill the reservoir of your airbrush. The lacquer is extremely thin, and it will splash out easily, so don't make any sudden movement, especially if you're using a gravity-feed brush.

Set your air supply's pressure to 12–15 psi and mist the model with the lacquer. Steadily move the airbrush 4"–6" above the surface until the entire model has an even mist layer. It's hard to see the effect with the first few passes, but as the paint builds up, the mirror-like

shine will become apparent, **32**. Don't forget to paint the wheel well doors and other pieces.

Tone variation. Alclad dries very quickly. This is great for applying multicolor metallic finishes because you can mask over it

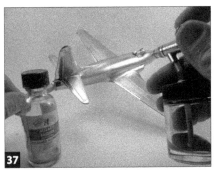

37

To refine the shine, I misted polished aluminum over the entire model.

38

Wait a little longer before spraying enamels or acrylics over the lacquer to avoid problems due to paint incompatibility.

39

Use decal-setting solutions sparingly to avoid marring the natural metal finish.

40

To be sure paint adheres, I sprayed the cast white metal gear legs with Tamiya metal primer, which goes on clear.

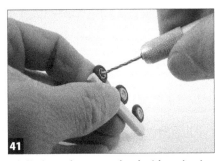

41

I drilled out the nose wheel with a pin vise to accept the axle. I used the pour plug as a handle during painting and preparation.

42

Don't forget the wheel wells. I brush-painted them zinc chromate primer acrylic. Mistakes are easy to wipe away.

43

Here's why it's call a sludge wash. The soap makes the mixtures a little thicker and it gets slopped on to the model.

44

To create light streaks, wipe the excess wash off the model in the direction of airflow.

45

I applied clear flat acrylic to the decals to dull their shine and give the warplane a realistic sheen.

within 30 minutes and spray individual panels with other Alclad shades, **33**. Don't press the tape into the surface too hard to minimize damage. I sprayed the center wing and stabilizer panels duraluminum, **34**. A few minutes after painting, I slowly removed the tape, pulling it back on itself, **35**. Then I masked and sprayed several panels white aluminum, **36**. Finally, to reduce the contrast a little and blend panels, I misted the model with polished aluminum, **37**. I waited until the next day to mask and spray the nose to avoid any conflict between the lacquer and the black enamel, **38**.

Applying clear gloss over Alclad will dull the shine. Fortunately, the paint is super smooth and takes decals perfectly. The manufacturer warns against using setting solutions because they mar the finish. I've had luck using Micro Sol on troublesome decals, but I apply the solution directly to the decal and immediately wipe off the surrounding surface with a cotton swab, **39**.

Landing gear. Scale Aircraft Conversions makes beautiful white metal landing gear legs. They are straight replacements for kit parts, have more refined detail than plastic parts, and have the strength to support heavy models. But the metal needs to be treated before painting. I primed SAC's F-80 legs with Tamiya metal primer, **40**.

After several hours, I brushed on Model Master aluminum and painted the oleos Model Master chrome silver.

I painted the True Details wheels while they were still attached to the pour plug; the hubs are Model Master aluminum and the tires Tamiya NATO black. The axle hole on the nose wheel was shallow to the point of being non-existent. I compared drill bits to the axle on the metal leg until I found a matching diameter and bored out the hub, **41**. The axles on the legs were too long, so I cut a little off and test-fit the wheels until the length was right. The wheel wells received a brush-painted coat of green zinc chromate, **42**.

46

The gun compartment doors on an F-80 got a lot of use. I painted chips in the markings around the hatch with dots of Model Master chrome silver.

47

I lightly dragged the tip of a hobby knife along the hatch outline to reveal the Alclad under the decal.

The Monogram 1/48 scale F-80 Shooting Star is the only option if you want a 1/48 scale model of this Korean War combatant. It builds into a nice replica with a little work and some extra details.

Weathering. Natural-metal airplanes don't fade or chip like their painted brethren, but they still suffer wear and tear, especially in war. I wanted to apply a wash to highlight the model's newly scribed panel lines, but the thin Alclad lacquer would be damaged by enamel thinner or turpentine used for oil washes. Instead, I used an acrylic sludge wash. I mixed a few drops of black and brown Tamiya acrylic paint into a tablespoon of water and then added a few drops of dishwashing detergent. The soap breaks up the surface tension of the water, so

the wash won't bead up on the surface. Then I brushed the mix onto the panel lines, **43**. Don't worry about staying in the lines; the excess will be removed in the next step.

Just like their oil counterparts, sludge washes are best applied to gloss paint for ease of removal. After a few minutes, wipe the model with a damp paper towel or a cloth, **44**. This will remove the paint from the surface but leave color in the engraved lines. Wipe in the direction air would flow over the airplane in flight so any streaks look natural.

I sprayed the glossy decals with a thin layer of clear flat to dull the shine, **45**. Set the nozzle to a narrow pattern and keep the pressure low (15 psi) to minimize overspray that may affect the finish. Finally, I chipped the paint around the nose by applying tiny dots and splotches of Model Master chrome silver along panel lines, especially around the gun access hatches, **46**. I added a few more scratches by gently scraping the decal with the point of a hobby knife, **47**. I added the landing gear, weapons, fuel tanks and canopy, and my F-80 was ready for another mission.

9

Building BIG FIGURES

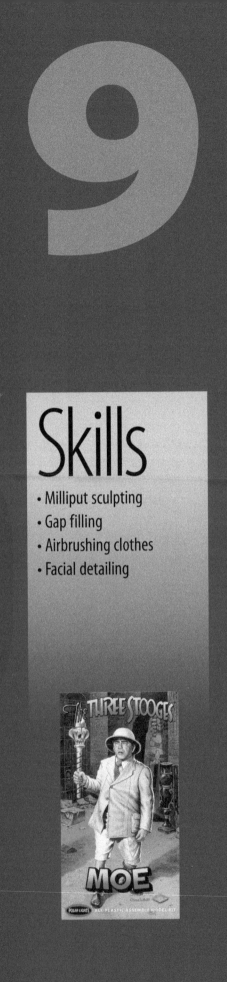

Skills

- Milliput sculpting
- Gap filling
- Airbrushing clothes
- Facial detailing

Large-scale figures have been an aspect of modeling almost since plastic models came on the market in the 1950s. Early industry colossus Aurora amused kids and freaked out parents with a long line of movie monsters as well as kits of people from history and popular culture. As a genre, big-figure modeling has had its ups and downs, but it seems to be experiencing something of a renaissance now. Manufacturers such as Moebius, Monarch, Round 2, and Pegasus have released beautiful figures with great sculpting and fits. Yet many modelers, myself included, shy away from the kits, worried that we can't paint them so they look good. But, you know, it's not as hard as it looks. Like any skill, it just takes practice.

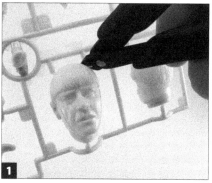

1

Figures have a lot of curves, and most body parts, such as Moe's head, are assembled from halves.

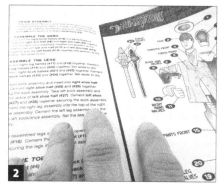

2

Instructions for many large-scale figure kits, perhaps by design, are a throwback to classic Aurora kits with a combination of narrative and illustrated instructions.

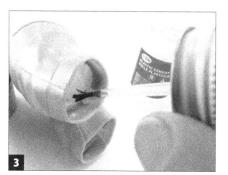

3

I slathered liquid cement on the inside of the joins to help fill the gaps.

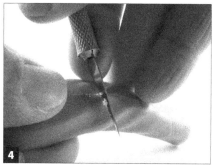

4

After scraping and shaving the bead of plastic that pushed out of the gap, you can see that most of the gap has been filled.

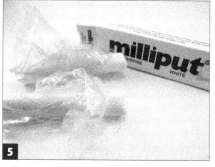

5

Milliput, a two-part epoxy putty, doesn't shrink as it dries, and it is easily sanded and sculpted when fully cured, so it's a good choice for filling seams on figures.

6

After combining equal parts of the putty's two parts, I kneaded the ball until it reached a uniform color.

BIG-SCALE FIGURES

During modeling's golden age of the 1950s and '60s, big-scale kits of historical and fictional characters were an important part of the hobby. Companies like Aurora, Lindberg, and Revell produced models of movie monsters, popular culture icons, animals, and even presidents. They proved popular with youthful builders, and many of the kits are now considered classics and fetch high prices among collectors.

The market seems to be enjoying a resurgence with new kits from manufacturers including Moebius, Monarch, and Pegasus, along with reissues from Revell and Round 2. Many of the new kits pay homage to Aurora, not only through subject selection, but in the design of the kit boxes and instructions. More than anything, big-scale kits emphasize fun.

Modelers have a wide choice of big-scale figures that includes reissues of Aurora classics like Vampirella and the Creature from the Black Lagoon and all-new molds such as Judge Dredd and Nosferatu.

Paging Dr. Howard. Committed to finishing a figure, I set upon Moe from The Three Stooges. One of three Polar Lights kits featuring the slapstick trio, the kit depicts Moe in safari gear holding a large torch (No. POL840), as seen in the 1938 film short "We Want Our Mummy." Moe's base is designed to fit together with those of Larry (No. POL839) and Curly (No. POL841), the other kits in the series.

Molded in off-white plastic, the kit features a good likeness of the perpetu-

ally scowling Moe, **1**. Just like the box art and the subject, the instructions are a throwback to classic Aurora figures. Instead of the mostly pictorial instructions included with many models, this model has written construction sequences complemented by a large exploded view diagram, **2**. This doesn't change the approach much, but it's important to read and follow the text instruction sequence to be sure you don't miss a step or a part.

Gluing and filling seams. There aren't a lot of parts in the kit, but unlike a vehicle, there are a lot of compound curves. Most of Moe's body parts are molded in halves, and none of those joins fall on clothing seams. So the challenge is getting the parts together and eliminating the seams. The easiest way to do this is by filling the gaps with plastic. I placed the major parts loosely together—you want enough of a gap so glue can run into it. Then, I liberally applied a slow-setting liquid cement like

7 Working with Milliput can be messy. Keep a little water nearby to prevent sticking and to help smooth and blend the putty over the joins.

8 You can use spatulas or craft sticks, but I find that fingers work best for getting the putty into gaps and seams.

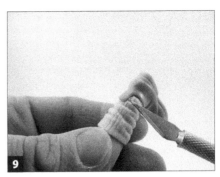

9 The tip of an old No. 11 blade proves useful for getting putty into tight spots without smearing the stuff around and filling detail.

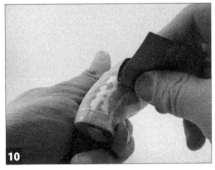

10 After 24 hours, sand the Milliput to reveal the plastic around the gaps. Be sure to follow the folds to prevent flat spots.

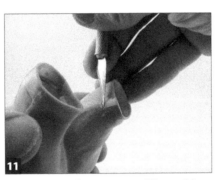

11 Remove putty from engraved lines with a hobby knife. Work slowly and try not to chip putty from areas where you want it to remain.

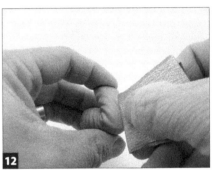

12 You can fold sandpaper and use the crease to smooth engraved detail.

13 Primer is essential to check for unfilled seams and blemishes. Mr. Surfacer 1000 does a good job of filling fine scratches and provides a smooth foundation for paint.

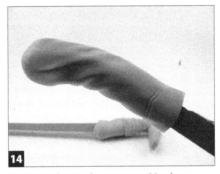

14 On bare plastic, the seam on Moe's arm seemed invisible. Under Mr. Surfacer 1000, it's obvious I need to do a little more work, which is why we prime.

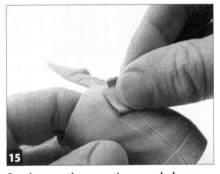

15 Sand across the seam. In several places, the primer was enough to eliminate the gap. I filled more persistent gaps with super glue.

Testors onto the join from behind, **3**. After 10–15 seconds, I pushed the parts tightly together. The pressure forced plastic melted by the solvent cement out of the gap. Once it dried, I trimmed it away with a sharp knife, **4**.

Milliput. There were still a few gaps that required work. I wanted a filler that would blend the edges of the join, make the seam disappear, and be easy to work with. Enter Milliput, a two-part epoxy putty, **5**.

To prepare, I roughed the area around the join with sandpaper to give the putty a firmer foothold. I kneaded equal amounts of the two parts with my fingers until the color was consistent, **6**. To avoid contamination, never use the same knife or tool to cut the epoxy components—there is nothing worse than pulling out the box the next time you need it and finding the putty ruined. Also, keep a little water handy; it'll stop the putty from sticking to your fingers and make it easier to work, **7**.

I applied more putty than necessary to fill each gap, pushing it along the seam with my finger, **8**. You can use other tools, but I find a wet fingertip manipulates the putty as well as anything. More water will blend and smooth the putty's edges and minimize sanding. I paid particular attention to the cuffs of Moe's shirt and shorts, building putty up front and back to be sure it was solid. With a knife tip, I forced putty into the small gaps, **9**. I let the filler dry overnight and then started sanding

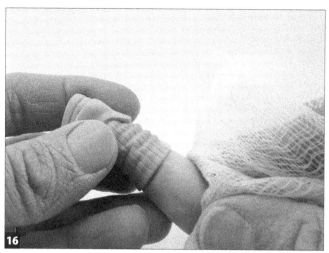

16

To remove sanding dust that may ruin paint, rub the parts with a tack cloth before the final primer coat.

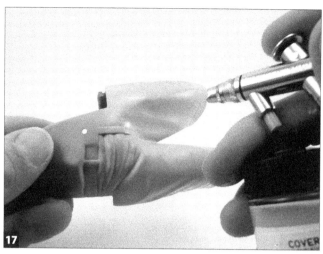

17

I sprayed the shorts with a base coat of Tamiya acrylics—buff and white—aiming for a uniform finish for the shading to come.

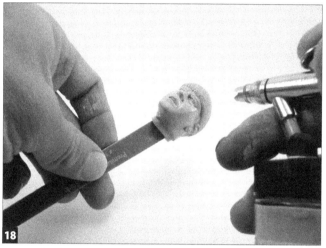

18

Tamiya flat flesh seemed a little garish straight from the bottle, so I added a little white and buff and sprayed Moe's head.

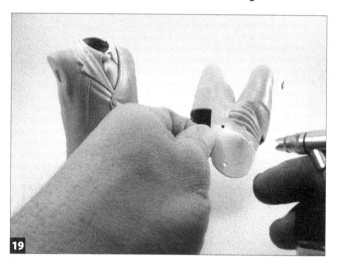

19

For contrast, I added a few drops of buff to white and airbrushed the shirt above the belt and at the collar of the jacket. The torso is unassembled at this point because it has to be built around the finished legs.

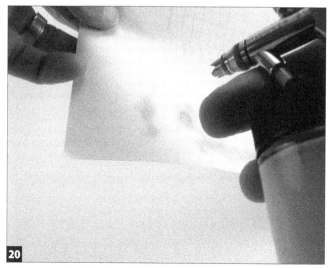

20

Before spraying fine lines for shading, test the spray pattern on paper. If you are using a single-action airbrush, you can fine-tune the needle placement. You want it fine, but paint has to spray.

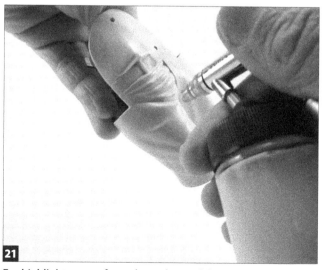

21

For highlights, spray from above the model, so the paint lands on surfaces exposed to direct light.

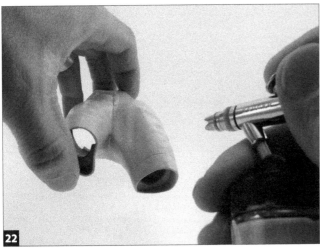

22 For shadows, airbrush a darker version of the base color under folds and in recesses. Don't panic if you get shading color where you don't want it. You can always correct it with a little of the original base color.

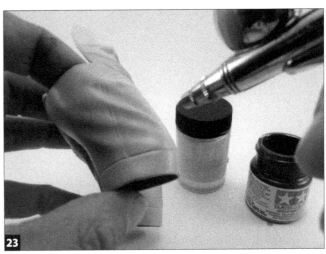

23 To enhance the effect, I mixed more brown into the base color and airbrushed finer lines into the deepest areas of shadow.

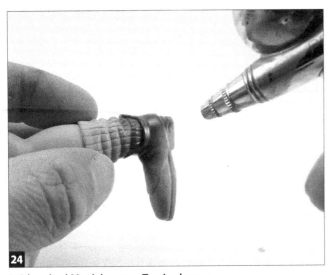

24 I airbrushed Moe's brogans Tamiya brown…

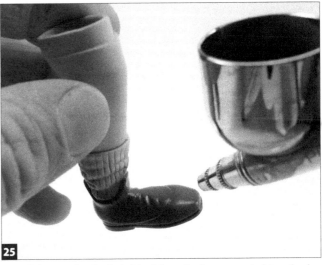

25 …and then I mixed a little black into the brown and airbrushed fine lines around recesses and the edge of the soles.

using 400-, 600-, and 1000-grit sandpaper, following the folds of the clothing across the seam, **10**. The point of a hobby knife, **11**, or sandpaper folded into a crease removed putty where engraved lines crossed the join, **12**.

Priming and re-priming. When working with figures, the finish is crucial. While most vehicles have seams and joints, human beings don't. The best way to check your finish is to prime the parts. I sprayed Moe with Mr. Surfacer 1000, but any primer will work, **13**.

After letting the primer dry for a few days, I checked the parts for inadequately filled seams and discovered that almost all of them could benefit from some extra

work, **14**. I sanded each seam initially with 400-grit sandpaper, rubbing until bare plastic was visible around most of the seams and any trace of the line was gone. I followed with 600- and 1000-grit sandpaper to smooth the surfaces and remove any scratches, **15**. A rubdown with a tack cloth removed the sanding dust, **16**. Finally, to check my work and establish a uniform surface for painting, I sprayed the parts with another layer of Mr. Surfacer 1000.

Painting. I started by painting the legs, hands, head, and shorts with Tamiya acrylics. I mixed buff and white and airbrushed Moe's shorts with a nice even coat, **17**. The flesh tones are a mix of 50 percent flat flesh, 25 percent buff, and 25 percent

white, **18**. The shirt is white with 25 percent buff, **19**. I stored the unused portions of each color for shading later.

After 24 hours, I lightened the shade used for the shorts with white, added a little more thinner, and adjusted the needle in the Badger 200 to a fine spray, **20**. I airbrushed this mix on creases and ridges, **21**. Imagine light coming from above the model—you can even use a lamp to produce a light source—and add this lighter shade where the light would strike the model directly. Unlike dry-brushing that hits the tips of raised detail, these highlights should be on one side of recesses. Because the paint is thin, you can build up the color's density, but be sure not to hold the

26 For the socks, I sprayed a mix of buff and wooden deck tan. Note the tape above the sock and the absence of any masking for the shoe.

27 I outlined diamonds with a 10/0 brush and a mix of red and black Tamiya acrylics. I varied the size and shape of the pattern slightly to account for the folds.

28 After painting the outlines, I filled each diamond with color. Using a little thinner kept the paint flowing smoothly over the molded detail.

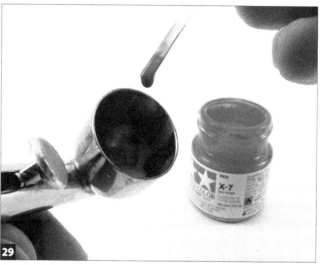

29 I switched to a double-action airbrush with a gravity-feed paint cup, so I could easily and quickly adjust the color and viscosity on the fly by adding a few drops of paint or thinner.

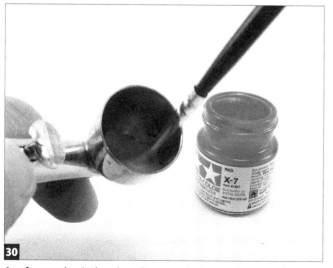

30 A soft, round paintbrush makes a perfect mixer because the bristles easily move paint around the paint cup.

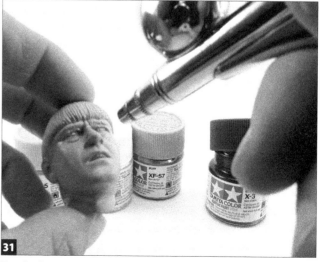

31 For shadows around Moe's face, I added a drop of royal blue to the base flesh color.

32 Adding a little red to the flesh tone brought color to Moe's cheeks and life to his face.

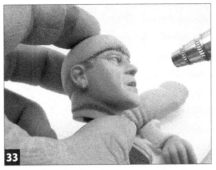

33 A little thin flesh color corrected red overspray and softened the contrasts.

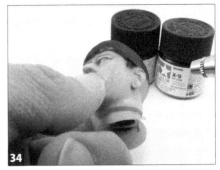

34 I airbrushed a mix of Tamiya black and brown for the hair and eyebrows.

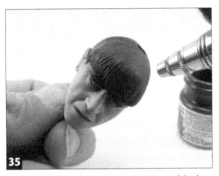

35 Light streaks of thin brown paint added more life to the hair and made it look less monolithic.

36 I mixed Tamiya flesh and red on a palette to paint Moe's lips.

37 When painting details, work slowly and carefully, using the molded detail to guide the brush.

38 Thin red paint flowed into the recessed detail darkens the mouth.

39 Use a light touch and thin paint to add more life to the flesh. Look at photos and faces for inspiration.

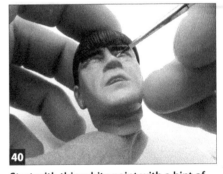

40 Start with thin white paint with a hint of the iris color (brown) and flow it into the eyes. Follow with slightly thicker paint.

airbrush in one place for too long or it will run.

I mixed a darker shade of the base color with more buff and thinner and sprayed under overhangs and other recesses, such as between the legs and the area the jacket would cover, **22**. Again imagine the light source when applying the paint. I deepened the shadows by adding Tamiya brown and more thinner to the mix and airbrushed finer lines in shadow areas, **23**.

Shoes and socks. I used straight brown for Moe's shoes, **24**, and then sprayed fine lines of brown mixed with black

along seams and the sole, **25**. I finished the shoes with a spot of brown mixed with white on the toes. After masking the legs with Tamiya tape, I airbrushed the socks with a mix of buff and deck tan, **26**. I didn't bother masking the boots. Instead, I airbrushed close to the leather, but left some of the brown at the join to serve as shadows. To give the socks an argyle look, I outlined diamonds with a fine-point brush and a mix of Tamiya red and black, varying each shape a little to suit the folds, **27**, and filled in each diamond, **28**. The finish was pretty shiny at this point, but a coat of clear flat at the end will fix that.

Focus on the face. Wanting a little more control, especially around the face, I switched to a double-action, gravity feed brush. Not only could I adjust the paint flow on the fly, but I could spray at very low pressure and alter the color in the paint cup for easy changes, **29** and **30**.

For shadows and creases in the flesh, I added a drop or two of Tamiya royal blue to the base flesh color and added more thinner, **31**. (Blue may seem an odd choice, but shadows on flesh tend to be more purple than black.) I sprayed it in the corners of the eyes, under the brow and chin, behind the ears, and along creases such as the ones from the corners of the

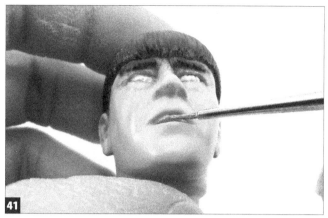

41

I used buff rather than white for the teeth, so they didn't look too stark on the face.

42

Next came the irises. I painted them brown, first by flowing thin brown paint into the recessed outline and then by painting the remainder of the circle with thicker paint.

43

Pupils should be the same size and centered within the iris. I used a fine-point brush and just enough paint.

44

No, this isn't a miniature Stooge eye poke. I used a toothpick to add white catchlights to Moe's eyeballs.

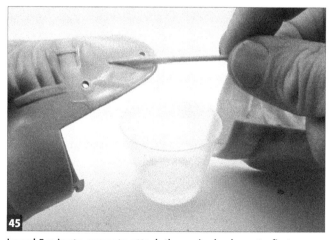

45

I used 5-minute epoxy to attach the major body parts, first smearing it onto the mating surfaces…

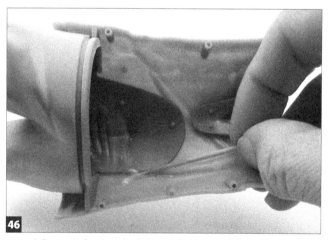

46

…and then reinforcing the joins with a bead of the adhesive inside.

nose to the mouth. Next, I added red and thinner to the base color to give Moe's cheeks a little color, **32**. If I got too much red in one place, I lightened the flesh shade and blended the colors, **33**. There's no magic art or rules here; I kept adding different flesh shades until it looked right.

I painted Moe's patented bowl-cut hairdo with a mix of Tamiya black and brown, **34**, and added streaks of brown following the engraved hair texture, **35**.

Eyes and mouth. In preparation for painting the mouth and other facial detail, I

put a little Tamiya flesh, red, royal blue, and thinner onto a palette, **36**. I painted the lips a mix of flesh and red using a fine brush and sticking to the molded outline, **37**. To darken the inside of the mouth, I flowed in a wash of thin red paint, **38**. While I had red and flesh on the palette, I

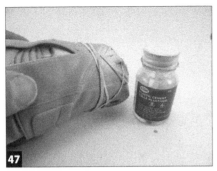

47 Rubber bands clamp the torso together while Testors liquid cement applied to the side seams dries.

48 I applied gap-filling cement to close seams at the collar and shoulders. Obviously, the shirt will have to be repainted.

49 I masked the shorts with kitchen foil and tape before painting the jacket.

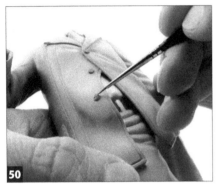

50 Vallejo acrylic paints brush beautifully with almost no brush strokes. I used them to add the buttons and belt.

51 Now that's styling! I brush-painted Moe's tie with Tamiya yellow and red. Work slowly and check your work often to keep the stripes even.

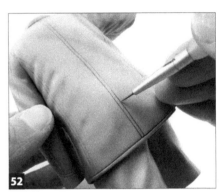

52 I flowed a wash of brown artist's oil and Turpenoid into the seam details and around the buttons and belt.

53 I used a mix of gloss and flat finishes on the figure, but a light application of Model Master Acryl clear flat toned down the shine and tied everything together.

54 How to start a fire: paint thin stripes of Tamiya clear red inside the clear torch halves near the base of the molded flames.

55 Tamiya clear orange and clear yellow finished the flames. For fun, I added clear yellow inside the eyes.

further blended the cheeks and nose with thin layers of color, **39**.

For the whites of Moe's eyes, I added a tiny bit of brown, the color I planned to use for the irises, and a little thinner and flowed that into the eyes with a fine brush, **40**. Plain white seemed too stark, and using the iris color blended everything together. (For the same reason, I used buff instead of white for the teeth, **41**.) I lightened brown a little with white and added thinner for better paint flow

and painted the irises, **42**. This kit has engraved iris outlines, which make painting them easy. Unfortunately, there are no outlines for the pupils, so you're on your own for painting them. I picked up a tiny dab of Tamiya black on a fine-point brush to paint the pupils, **43**. The important thing to remember is to center the pupil in the iris. I dilated Moe's to fit with the figure's fearful pose. The final touch was adding little dots of white in each eye for catchlights, spots of reflected light that

give figures life. I dipped a round toothpick in a shallow pool of Tamiya white and then touched it to the eyes, above and to the right of the center, **44**. Don't center catchlights, but make sure they are in the same place in each eye.

Body assembly and painting. I was worried about the connection between the upper legs and the torso because the joining surfaces were relatively small. I used 5-minute epoxy to attach the components and reinforce the connection. After mixing equal amounts of both epoxy parts, I applied some to the joining surface on the shirt front, **45**, pressed the parts together, and held them for five minutes to ensure a tight fit. To be sure the connection was solid, I added epoxy to the inside of the join, **46**. I used epoxy to glue the back half to the legs, but flowed liquid cement into the gaps on the jacket to join the front and back and help fill the seams, **47**. I used epoxy to make sure the shirt collar parts stayed together and then used gap-filling super glue to eliminate several seams, **48**.

After masking the legs, I painted the jacket Tamiya wooden deck tan. I then added shadows with thin mixes of deck tan and brown as well as highlights with thin mixes of deck tan and white, **49**. I painted the buttons with Vallejo new wood and his belt Vallejo leather belt brown, **50**. I touched up Moe's shirt collar by hand and painted the tie yellow with red stripes applied with a fine brush, **51**. Finally, I added a red brown artist's oil wash to the seams in the figure's clothes, **52**.

After adding the head, hands, and feet with 5-minute epoxy, I toned down the shine and blended everything together with a coat of Model Master Acryl clear flat, **53**. I flowed a little Tamiya clear into the eyes to give them a wet sheen.

Lighting the torch. Polar Lights supplies Moe's torch in two clear parts, including the flames. Before gluing the halves together, I painted the flames inside the parts, starting with a few streaks of Tamiya clear red, **54**. Streaks of clear orange and a coat of clear yellow followed; I concentrated the darker colors at the base of the flames, **55**.

After gluing the halves together and cleaning up the join with super glue filler and sanding, I painted the body of the torch with Testors gold enamel and painted the engraved detail on the handle black. I inserted the torch in Moe's hand and the chief Stooge was ready for his Egyptian expedition.

Big-scale figures aren't as hard as they seem—I did most of the delicate painting and blending with airbrushes—and the finished model gets a lot of attention from modelers and nonmodelers alike.

Boo! Figures don't have to be scary. They're just like any other model—a collection of parts and subassemblies. And there are some fun subjects available, including **The Three Stooges.**

DISPLAYING
your model

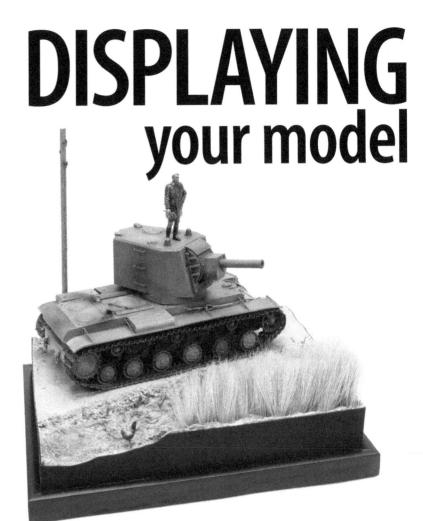

So far, all of the projects in this book have ended with a model sitting on a shelf. There's nothing wrong with that except that the subject is out of context. You can convey a lot about a model by placing it in a scene.

For example, the USS *Cole* from Chapter 6 looks okay on the shelf, but imagine the ship plowing through an ocean, cutting a sharp bow wave, or pitching up on rough seas. With the Tiger tank in Chapter 7, the heavy weathering gives a sense of the tough winter conditions around Leningrad. However, place the model on a snowy base with a figure bundled against the cold, and even the most casual observer will shiver in appreciation of the severe conditions. Even aircraft can benefit from display work. I plan to place the F-80 from Chapter 8 in a Korean War revetment, being readied for another mission.

1 Given the tank's size, an 8" x 10" frame seemed the perfect size. I took the glass and cardboard backing out, but saved the clips to secure the base.

2 I laid the frame's cardboard backing over foam core and cut around it with a hobby knife to form a base for the groundwork.

3 I ran masking tape around the frame to keep the black metal clean and looking sharp during the messy earthwork-making process to come.

4 I placed the KV on the base. Note that it is at an angle to the edges and off center.

5 Using a permanent marker, I sketched out the perimeter of the road as well as the ditch and pasture.

6 In addition to being light and strong, insulating foam is easy to work with. After being sliced part way through, a piece can be easily broken and leave a clean edge.

Bases are not hard, and they are a great way to display your finished model. The main thing to remember, as with any modeling project, is to be willing to try something new and have fun.

Setting the KV. After building the KV tank in the first chapter, I decided to place it in a scene. I knew my scene would probably be set in summer 1941 around the time of the German invasion of the Soviet Union. I was also limited

by having already built the kit and fixing the suspension, so the ground would have to be flat underneath the running gear. Also, the hatches were glued shut, so I couldn't place a figure in the tank. After playing around with a couple of ideas, I settled on placing the tank on a narrow dirt road overlooking a ditch and field. The road and ditch would run diagonally across the base from corner to corner with the field in one of the other corners.

KV TANKS

More than 500 KV heavy tanks were in Red Army service when Germany invaded the Soviet Union in June 1941. The KV-1's armor proved too much for the 7.5cm and 5cm main guns mounted on German Panzer III and IV tanks, while it's 76.2mm main gun was powerful enough to penetrate most enemy armor in service at the time. Unfortunately, the tank proved to be too heavy for many bridges in the Soviet Union. It was also difficult to steer, and its transmission was unreliable.

A preserved KV-1 is on display at the U.S. Army Aberdeen Proving Ground museum.

The massive KV-2, armed with a 152mm howitzer in an oversize turret, was designed as a slow-moving artillery tank for use against fixed emplacement and bunkers. The KV-2 was heavier, and the turret was difficult to traverse when the vehicle was on a slope, making the tank top-heavy. Usually deployed in small numbers, the effectiveness of KV tanks can be difficult to pin down, but there are stories of small groups destroying dozens of German tanks. The arrival of German Tigers and Panthers on the Eastern Front in 1942 and '43 provided the impetus for a new Soviet heavy tank, which became the IS-2.

Framing the foundation. If you visit a model show, you'll see models displayed on many different types of bases. I decided to build a base using a relatively basic method cribbed from model railroading. The first step is constructing a base for the groundwork. One of the most basic foundations is a wood plaque or even just an appropriately sized piece of wood. If you use wood, you'll need to seal it with varnish or polyurethane to prevent moisture from warping the base. Use the models to determine the right size and shape needed. Traditionalists believe that no

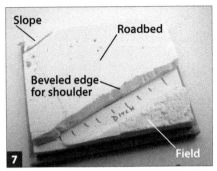

Slope
Roadbed
Beveled edge for shoulder
Ditch
Field

7 To finalize the scene's topography, I added the surface for the field as well as the edge of the road across the way.

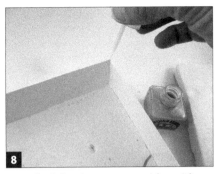

8 I attached the sheet styrene sides with liquid cement. Be careful not to drip any on the foam—it'll eat it alive, dissolving your hard work.

9 I used white glue to attach the foam to the base. Toothpicks pushed through the upper layers into the base prevent the pieces from moving as the glue dries.

10 You can use a spoon or craft stick to mix Sculptamold, but I prefer using my fingers to thoroughly knead the elements together.

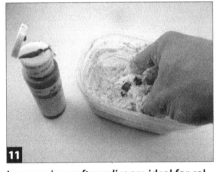

11 Inexpensive craft acrylics are ideal for coloring the groundwork mix. It may not be the final color, but it helps disguise chips and scratches on the finished base.

12 I added white glue to the mix to ensure that it would stick to the foam and also help rocks and vegetation adhere.

part of a vehicle should extend past the edge of the base. Don't be afraid to think outside the box; extending the action past the edge can heighten the drama of the scene.

For the KV, my aim was to keep things simple and stick with readily available supplies. To that end, I used a metal picture frame as the frame for the base, **1**. The cardboard backing served as a template for cutting foam core that I clipped into the frame, **2**. Groundwork involves plaster or papier-mâché and paint. In other words, it's messy, so tape the edge of the base to protect it from spills and splatters, **3**. Next, I cut a 1"-thick piece of insulating foam board—it usually comes in pink or blue and is available from home improvement stores—to fit inside the frame. The lightweight foam is dense and strong yet is easily cut and carved. Remember that it will be slightly smaller than the foam core to account for the frame's overlap. I attached the foam to the foam core with white glue.

Roadwork and ditch digging. The top of this initial piece of foam will be the lowest point on the final display—the bottom of the ditch—so the road and field needed to be built on top of it. To plan the road's location, I placed the model on the base, **4**. Then I marked the position of the major components, **5**.

I trimmed a piece of foam for the roadbed, shaving the edges at an angle to produce a sloped shoulder. The foam is easily cut by passing a hobby knife along a line and grasping it firmly on either side, breaking it along the incision, **6**. I carved a smaller section of foam to raise the field above the ditch but not to the same elevation as the road, **7**. At the opposite corner, I added a wedge of foam to produce a gentler slope at the edge of the road. Keep in mind that none of the foam work has to be perfect; the groundwork to come will fill gaps and smooth over any rough patches. Before permanently attaching the extra foam, I built a wall of .040" sheet styrene around the base to serve

as a retaining wall for the groundwork, **8**. Finally, I attached the foam for the road with white glue and set it aside to dry for several hours, **9**.

Getting dirty. I've used Celluclay and plaster as groundwork, but I prefer Sculptamold, a lightweight papier-mâché mix that is activated with water, **10**. Add acrylic paint to the mix, choosing colors that best represent the area being modeled, such as sand for desert, dark earth for southern Russia, or reddish brown for Vietnam, **11**. I used inexpensive craft acrylics for the KV's base, kneading the paint into the Sculptamold by hand. The final ingredient is a generous dollop of white glue to help the groundwork stick to the base, **12**. Remember that adding liquids, like the paint and glue, will affect consistency. You need the mix to be thin enough to work by hand but thick enough to hold form and shape over slopes. Mix it in a plastic container that you don't mind throwing away after you're done.

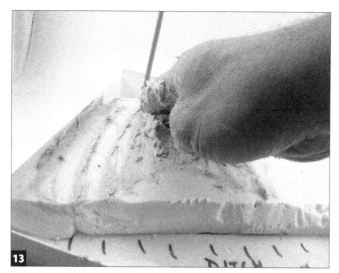

13 Hands are ideal for applying Sculptamold to the base.

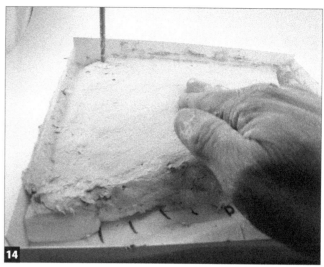

14 I dipped my fingers in water to smooth the surface of the road. Thin layers dry quickly.

15 While the groundwork is still wet, I pushed the vinyl tank tracks into the surface in order to leave their impression.

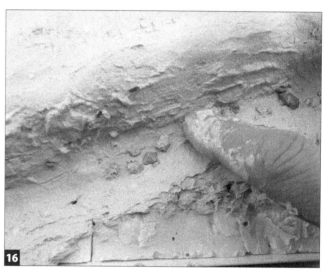

16 Kitty litter—unused is best—makes great rocks in 1/35 scale. The clay chunks are realistically shaped and inexpensive.

17 I pushed toothpicks through the Sculptamold and into the foam to plant grass and flowers in the ditch. Note the play sand used as gravel along the side of the road.

18 A chisel blade works well to remove unwanted high spots.

DIORAMA DESIGN THEORY

Whether you want a base to go around a model or you have an idea for a diorama to build from the ground up including figures, take time to design it before mixing groundwork. There are no right or wrong answers, but here are a few guidelines that will improve even the simplest base. Have a story or purpose. Think about what you want to say. Are you building the base to give the subject context? Or are you trying to tell a larger story or illustrate a theme?

Keep it simple. It's easy to get going and think that dioramas need multiple vehicles and a ton of figures. But the truth is that less is more. Most of the best displays I've seen are smaller, simpler affairs that convey their message loud and clear.

Maintain focus. Know what you want to say or show and remove any items or figures that distract from the scene or story.

Avoid parallel lines. Don't align the scene's elements with the frame. In other words, if you have a road or runway in the scene, position it diagonally on the base rather than running it parallel to the sides. This makes the diorama visually dynamic.

Don't center the subject. Place the main elements closer to a side or corner, not in the middle of the base. Photographers and artists use the rule of thirds to make images more appealing. Divide the scene into thirds with imaginary lines drawn on both axes and place the major elements on those lines or intersections.

Use balance, not symmetry. Elements should complement each other on the base, but you don't want one side to mirror the other. If you have a fighter in an airfield scene with a ground crew, don't space the figures evenly around the aircraft. Group them to focus attention and balance other elements such as vehicles.

Break the vertical plane. Place subjects on rises or banks rather than flat surfaces. It gives the impression of movement and action to the scene.

Think outside the box. Don't be afraid to try something different. The most interesting and dynamic dioramas are the ones that force the viewer to look at it a second time. You can find ideas and inspiration in *FineScale Modeler* or at model shows.

Chris Toops built Respite to show the crew of an M12 self-propelled gun at rest. None of the elements in the scene are parallel to base's borders. The vehicle is close to the center, but the balance of the details, including the figures, shells, and walls are balanced around it without being symmetrical. And all the figures help tell the story of soldiers' downtime between missions. *FineScale Modeler photo*

The base for Richard Guetig's M113A2 is the epitome of simple, and it is just big enough for the vehicle, but it achieves one important thing—it breaks the vertical plane. By posing the armored personnel carrier on a slope, Richard gave the vehicle a sense of drama and action. *FineScale Modeler photo*

19

I airbrushed the ground with a mix of tan and yellow-brown based on photos of soil from the western regions of Russia and Belarus, where I set the scene.

20

Dry-brushing the foliage adds variety to the rather uniform model-railroad products.

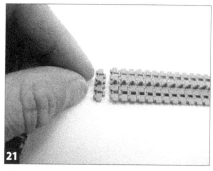

21

I detached and cleaned up the Trumpeter kit's individual track links and then pushed them together.

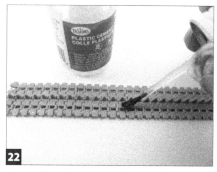

22

Testors liquid cement is the perfect slow-setting adhesive for attaching track links. It allows you to form the tracks around the running gear.

23

Use a few books to press the KV into the base as the 5-minute epoxy sets. Don't use too much weight, so you don't damage the suspension. Note the trimmed and painted styrene edges.

24

Pastels or weathering pigments give the ground a dry, dusty appearance and tie the vehicle and groundwork together.

Now you're ready to slap the earth down. You can use tools, but I prefer my hands, so I can feel the relative thickness of the Sculptamold mix as I place it, **13**. I started by making the road flat so it could accommodate the tank's running gear; I pushed a handful at a time into place in the foam and worked it over the foam. You can smooth the Sculptamold with wet fingers so keep a tub of water handy, **14**. While the surface is still wet, push tracks, wheels, or feet into the ground, **15**.

Rocks and vegetation. After creating the road, I applied Sculptamold to the ditch. Imagining the way water flows and erodes earth, I spent less time trying to make the sides and bottom even. I pushed bits of clean cat litter into the Sculptamold along the bottom of the ditch, **16**. I prefer cat litter to the rocks and gravel sold for model railroads because the latter tends to be a little too uniform in size and shape. I sprinkled play sand along the shoulders and in the ditch to represent smaller stones and pebbles.

On the other hand, model railroad sources are great places to find flora for dioramas. I used Busch HO scale grain field and reeds (HO7375) for the straw and the stray grass along the road and used HO scale goldenrods for flowers. To plant the vegetation along the ditch, I pushed a toothpick through the still-wet Sculptamold and into the foam, **17**. Remember that nature is rarely uniform when placing vegetation. Vary the size of clumps and don't space them evenly. For the field, I pushed larger clumps of the Busch grain into the Sculptamold mix and then pushed the earth tight around the plant bases. Later, I squirted white glue into the grass to be sure it stuck. After the groundwork dries, invert the base and shake it gently to remove any unattached scenery.

More detail and color. One of the great things about Sculptamold is that in can be carved, sanded, and drilled after it dries, which makes refining shapes easy. After testing the fit of the KV, I discovered

a couple of high spots. I removed them using a chisel blade in a hobby knife handle and some light sanding, **18**.

Coloring the mix helps shade the ground, but painting adds tone variation and ties the elements together. I airbrushed a mix of yellow-brown and tan over the road and then darkened the paint slightly to cover the ditch and shoulders. I added patches and stripes of lighter and darker tones to the road, **19**. Don't paint the plants but don't be afraid to get a little paint on the base of the vegetation; it'll look like a light coat of dust. Before ending the painting session, I added a little clear flat and thinner to the dirt color and airbrushed a coat of dust onto the tank's running gear and lower hull. This helps tie the model and groundwork together.

It's a good idea to step back from the base occasionally and look at what you have. It's easy to get lost in the details and not see the whole scene. After painting the groundwork, I thought it needed more vegetation to look like mid-summer in the

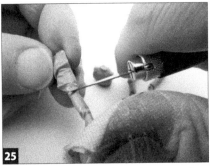

25

I scraped mold seams from the parts of a MiniArt Soviet tanker with a hobby knife. Note the bandage: did I mention hobby knives are sharp?

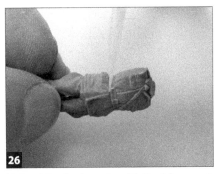

26

I joined the body parts with liquid cement and used a little super glue to fill minor gaps and blend the clothing.

27

I base-coated the leather jacket with NATO black…

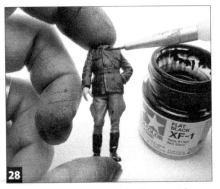

28

…and then picked up shadows with flat black. Highlights were painted with Panzer gray.

29

The figure serves to give the tank scale, and the rooster gives a sense of rural calm. Plus it let me finish a model given to me by my sister.

western Soviet Union. I brushed patches of white glue along the edge of the ditch and road shoulder. I picked a package with several shades of green, but color choice is not critical because I applied a heavy layer of dry-brushed yellow green, **20**. Finally, I trimmed the styrene edging and airbrushed it flat black.

Tracks. I replaced the tank's vinyl tracks with the styrene link-and-length tracks. Individual and link-and-length tracks can be daunting. Here's how I do it: First, clean up each link and push them together to form two or three runs on each side, **21**. For the KV, I used the molded top run as one and formed a single run for the bottom, front, and back. Then, brush a slow-setting liquid cement on the inside face of the runs, ensuring that the cement runs into each gap, **22**. Push the links firmly together. Let the lengths set for 15–20 minutes. They should hold together but be flexible. Next, wrap the lengths around the running gear, making sure each fits snugly

around the idlers and drive sprockets and that the ends meet. Lightly tape them in place if necessary and set the model aside overnight. After the glue has set solid, you should be able to pop the lengths off the model for painting and weathering and then reinstall them with super glue.

Attaching the model. I used 5-minute epoxy to secure the KV to the base. After applying a generous bead to each track link, I positioned the model on the base. A few books helped push the model into the surface so the track fit just right, **23**. Modelers who prefer a wooden base will often secure the model with a bolt running through the base and into the tank hull. Aircraft and figures can be held in place with bits of wire or pins glued into the base and inserted into holes in the wheels or feet. My final step was to brush pigments (pastels work too) over the groundwork and model, further reinforcing the connection between the elements, **24**.

Figures. Even a simple display like the KV benefits from a figure or two. It gives the model a sense of scale as well as conveying a sense of the vehicle's purpose. I picked a Soviet tank officer from a Miniart set. Most small scale styrene figures will have mold seams, **25**, but they are easy to construct, **26**.

I left the head separate for easier painting. I brushed on a layer of Model Master wood enamel and then painted highlights—chin, lips, nose, cheeks, and forehead—with Model Master tan. After painting the eyebrows with a fine line of Italian dark brown, I applied a tiny dot in the eyes to mark the pupils. Don't use any white in the eyes on 1/35 scale figures—it's too stark. A coat of clear flat and a wash of raw umber oil finished the flesh.

I prefer acrylics for clothing. I base-coated the tanker's trousers Tamiya khaki and his leather jacket NATO black, **27**. I applied flat black with a 10/0 brush for shadows under folds, collars, and pockets on the jacket, **28**. Panzer gray provided highlights. I altered khaki with yellow and green for highlights and shadows on the pants.

Final steps. For fun, and to reinforce the idea of rural peace before the storm (the German invasion), I painted a rooster from Tamiya's 1/35 scale livestock set, **29**. The rooster and figure were added to the scene with 5-minute epoxy.

The final step is adding a name plate—a black-and-white decal applied to sheet styrene and glued to the base—so the viewer instantly knows when and where the diorama is set.

About the Author

Aaron Skinner built his first model—some kind of racecar in white plastic—when he was 5, and he has had at least one model under construction ever since. Aaron grew up in Australia building a lot of Matchbox and Airfix 1/72 scale World War II aircraft, but his modeling interests have broadened to include armor—especially Russian stuff—1/48 scale aircraft, airliners, and science fiction spacecraft. He studied journalism and history at the University of Queensland in Brisbane, Australia, and worked as a photographer at newspapers in Texas and Arkansas before joining *FineScale Modeler* in 2006 as an associate editor.

Lightning Source UK Ltd.
Milton Keynes UK
UKHW050923160921
390667UK00001B/5